# PRAYER LITE

## IT'S WAY EASIER TO PRAY THAN YOU THINK

*Prayer made EASY for all faiths…Or… no faith.*

by Dr. Jarvis Endicott Williams

Copyright © 2022 by Dr. Jarvis Williams, DVM

All rights reserved. This book or any portion thereof may not be reproduced or used in any manner whatsoever without the express written permission of the publisher except for the use of brief quotations in a book review.

Publishing Services provided by Paper Raven Books LLC

Printed in the United States of America

Second Edition: 2022

Hardcover ISBN: 978-1-7379167-5-8
Paperback ISBN: 978-1-7379167-4-1

Visit www.jarviswrites.page for links to more books
by Jarvis Endicott Williams.
Or find them all on Amazon, Nook, etc.

Non-fiction books by the author are:
*Feeding Your Dog and Cat, The Truth!*
*Prayer Lite*

For thriller/mystery/crime-fiction/suspense/
humor books, try these titles:
*Dirty Money*
*A Rum With a View*

# CONTENTS

Chapter 1: Introduction.................................1

Chapter 2: Do You Have Prayer Neurosis?

        Spiritual Indigestions?.......................7

Chapter 3: Common Reasons to Pray....................11

Chapter 4: Prayer Works................................39

Chapter 5: How to Pray Out Loud—Even If You're Shy.....43

Chapter 6: Meditation: Inquire Within ..................51

Chapter 7: Prayer and Science .........................65

Chapter 8: The Lord's Prayer ..........................71

Chapter 9: Get Your Body into It .......................75

Chapter 10: When and Where to Pray ...................79

Chapter 11: Unintended Consequences May Happen

        When You Pray ...........................97

Chapter 12: It Will Be Good...........................101

Afterword ..........................................105

Appendix One Toxic Relationships ....................109

You want to get in touch with God…
You want to pray but don't know how…
It's been too long…
It doesn't get through unless you know *the language*…
You don't even know how to begin…

**After reading the first seven pages of this little book, you will be praying.**

*IT'S WAY EASIER TO PRAY
THAN YOU THINK*

# CHAPTER ONE

I longed for something to help me make sense of my life.

I just wanted to talk to God. Maybe ask for some help. Say the sunset was "awesome."

I longed for a sense of spirituality.

I wanted to pray.

Books on prayer were just collections of prayers. My attention drifted faster than I could turn the page. There was no simple formula for me to get started.

Lots of kids pray like a TV evangelist! I can't even begin.

In church, I didn't know where we were in the "program" half the time.

I tried different churches.

Authority figures told me I was born a sinner! Like from my first breath?

That there was only one way to God—their way.

I'd been wavering between doubt and faith my

whole life.

I felt stupid trying to pray. Am I just talking to myself?

I thought there were strict rules, a secret formula, or that I had to learn a language.

I felt like my prayers were just bumping against the ceiling like a balloon.

I wasn't sure I even believed in God, so maybe I wasn't allowed to pray.

Maybe I shouldn't call attention to myself—just stay under the radar (lightning).

Knowing myself as I do, I wondered why God would even care about me.

***Then God talked to me at three in the morning and I was forever changed. He said…***

"There are no rules."

"I'm easy to talk to."

"Don't make it like learning a new language."

"You don't even have to talk."

"You can babble incoherently; I'll understand."

"You can keep it simple."

"A word or phrase is enough."

"You cannot pray a prayer incorrectly."

"Besides, I grade on a curve."

"Silly, angry, shallow prayers are fine. You don't need to 'wow' me."

"I can help; I just need you to ask."

"In fact, you're praying right now."

So, I tried one:

I asked for help with the **Problem-of-the-day**.

I thanked Him for my bed…

and if He'd let me get some sleep...
I would think HE was the GREATEST!

I slept really well, and when I woke up, I didn't care as much about the Problem-of-yesterday (mostly because I thought of a new one for today. Still...).

So, I thanked God, and asked for help with every problem I had.

(All-inclusive-every-single-problem—I didn't elaborate.) And if He would help me, I would think He-was-the-greatest!

I realized I had prayed to be able to pray and that I was *actually praying*!

I ended up praying all day (kind of):

- "Help me get this work done. Thanks for being there for me. You're the greatest."
- "Help me not fall asleep. Thanks for helping me concentrate. I can't do it without you."
- "Help me have a great meeting. Thanks for providing the opportunity for us to get together. You are awesome."
- "Thanks for the great food. Help me use it for good. You're really great to provide so much for me."

That night, again at three in the morning, I woke up realizing that praying was simple!

All I had to do is ask Him for help, be thankful, and while I'm at it, probably add a "praise the Lord."

I realized that I had a "formula" for prayer that I could share:

1. **"PLEASE HELP!"**
2. **"THANK YOU!"**
3. **"GOD, YOU'RE GREAT!"**

It's way easier to pray than I thought! I should tell people about it. How easy it can be!

These three parts can make anything a prayer. It can fit any situation you can think of.

Or, you can use just one part. Like the "help" part. You don't have to use all three parts.

Or, you can just babble like a baby.

You can say anything you want (or: moan, groan, wail, cry, whimper, whine, snivel, whisper, or complain).

*(That's it. Now you know enough to get started. You can put the book back on the shelf and not even buy it.)*

THERE ARE NO RULES FOR A PRAYER:

- It doesn't have to be in "prayer-eze."
- It doesn't have to be aimed toward a certain address.
- It doesn't need a beginning or end.
- Your theology doesn't have to be right.
- You don't have to sound Biblical.
- You can do it on your own. You don't have to have a professional lead you.
- You don't need to know who you are praying to, why you want to pray, or what you want to say. You can say one word, dozens, or hundreds. You can take a second, or a whole day.
- You can pray to be able to pray.

- You don't have to be "centered" or be "one" with the universe. Or in some "holy" state of mind. In fact, you can be angry, insolent, bitchy, condescending, whiny, confused, drunk, lonely, tired, jilted, nasty, stubborn, depressed, suicidal, homicidal, or at a recital.
- You can be cutting the grass, driving the car, petting the dog, playing golf, shoveling snow, watching TV, applying for a loan, or on the throne.
- You don't have to be burning incense, fingering a rosary, crossing your heart, chanting, canting, ranting, be baptized, or circumcised.
- You don't have to pray for a particular outcome. (In fact, nonspecific, short prayers with open-ended requests, may even be the best! Martin Luther said, "The fewer words, the better prayer.")
- It can be just a thought, a feeling, or even just a yearning.
- It can even be an action. Hug, handshake, opening the door for someone, waiting in line patiently, a friendly wave, etc.
- You can just whine and moan about anything even if it doesn't make sense.

Picture an infant sitting on a parent's lap babbling. The child doesn't have to know how to talk for the parent to know what he or she wants. Picture yourself sitting on God's lap as a child. You can babble like a baby. He understands what you are trying to say, just like the parent.

And so, if prayers don't require words, and if a groan, or a kind action, can be a prayer, then why be afraid of trying it?

You cannot pray a prayer wrong.

*Again, you can put the book **back on the shelf**. You know all you need already.*

# CHAPTER TWO

**Do you have *Prayer Neurosis? Spiritual Indigestion?***

Dr. Larry Dossey, in his incredibly comprehensive book on prayer, Healing Words,[1] defines his term "Prayer Neurosis" as, "The result of struggling with, or trying to conform to, a certain prayer style that just doesn't work for you, or may make you so uncomfortable you avoid prayer entirely."

He believes you may recoil at being told how to pray a certain way because for you, the wording is complicated, stylized, or phony sounding. It can be like a foreign language; or like reading Shakespeare. Somehow you took to heart that prayer can only be done a certain way, and you are kind of neurotic about it and feel inadequate, maybe even a little guilty about

---

[1] Healing Words, The Power of Prayer and the Practice of Medicine; Harper, San Francisco, 1993; Larry Dossey MD.

your malfunction. So, you don't pray—prayer neurosis.

Some people develop an actual phobia regarding church and religion. Maybe you consider your formative years' church experience as "child abuse." (Sitting quietly in a suit, not having a clue what is going on, or worse). Maybe you deliberately avoid thoughts, feelings, activities, situations, and people that arouse your recollections of church as a kid.

Maybe the minister told you, "Pack your bags born sinner, you're going on a *guilt trip*. (And you didn't think you'd done enough sinning yet—you were just a kid after all—to be in that much trouble! You'd been kind of looking forward to a little sinning, in fact.)

Or God was described as a vindictive father figure, and so prayer for you came out scary, and far from comforting. You're afraid of God.

Or you were told there was only one religion in the world, and only its way was the right way, and you don't buy into that. There are lots of religions… and so they can't pray to God? (By the way, in Jerusalem's old walled city three major religious faiths coexist peacefully: Judaism, Muslim, and Christianity!)

The truth is: all roads lead to God.

The Bible has something to say about this: "For there is no difference between Jew and Gentile—the same Lord is Lord of all and richly blesses all who call on Him, for, 'Everyone who calls on the name of the Lord will be saved.'" (Romans 10; 12-13.)

Some have trouble with the word *god*. They associate the word with the image of a vindictive, scary, unforgiving, father figure. Or, they just can't get their minds around the traditional concept of God and creationism; it is too simplified and allegorical. Some are so beat up by life they can't believe there is a benevolent God. They no longer trust and have given up. Maybe are even contemplating suicide.

I had trouble with this... the word god. Someone said to just pick a tree or a rock or a law of physics. Or you can pray to the "Big Bang" theory. Or some quantum mechanics theory. Or gravity. (That's plenty mysterious.) Or an image of the swirling ethers from the Hubble telescope. Pray to anything just to get started. God's hanging around everywhere anyway.

It's between you and something bigger than you. And almost everything is bigger than you in some way. I am mystified by practically everything. I am awed by an ant. As long as you believe that there is something greater than yourself, even if you don't have a clear definition, or image of it, you have something to pray to.

This concept of something greater than oneself is beyond description anyway. That includes gender. (God is female?) So why try to describe God? Maybe someone else can describe God, but I can't. Just pray to a "Higher Power" and leave it at that.

Not only do you not have to name your higher power, you don't even have to be a 100 percent believer in God to pray. (I'm not a 100 percent anything.) And, you don't have to believe 100 percent in the power of prayer. You don't have to believe in anything to pray. You don't have to learn faith to pray.

Your Eminence... Oh Merciful Father... Your Awesomeness? You don't have to use fancy salutations.

It's like learning to walk; just take a step in any direction.

Totally turned off by traditional religions? You can explore other cultures to help you find a direction; American Indian drumming and chanting, Islamic Sufi dancing, Buddhist meditation, or Hindu Yoga. ("Sacrifice" is out these days, by the way. Well, not everywhere. We're big on personal sacrifice, aren't we?)

God understands there are many roads. They all lead to Him, no matter which you choose. One way or another He made all roads. In fact, you can even skip the "Who" part, and just start. Just figure it isn't you, and that there is something out there bigger than you, and jump right in.

Just say Hi!

God is multinational, multicultural, and multilingual. (God loves diversity.) Don't get hung up on salutations. He doesn't need to be told who he is.

As long as you believe that there is something beyond human understanding... something bigger than you... you have something to pray to.

There aren't any words that do Him justice anyway.

***PRAYER TIP #1: Just say "Hi." Then ask for what you want. Or say thanks. Couldn't be any simpler than that.***

# CHAPTER THREE

**PRAY FOR
HELP
FORGIVENESS
OTHERS
TO LET GO
RELATIONSHIPS
SENSE OF LACK
HELP WITH ANGER
THANKS
A REALITY CHECK**

**PRAYING FOR HELP:**
No matter what the suffering du jour is, prayer is always there to ask for help.

You can ask for help for anything. Help to get out of bed in the morning when it's cold and rainy, and you're afraid to go to work or class. Help to fall asleep.

Help to even find a bed. Help to make the bed (an anti-laziness prayer). You can ask for help getting through traffic, finding a parking place, going to the doctor, fixing dinner, putting the kids to bed, finding your keys, and certainly when you're lost.

(Lost soul… or really lost?)

It's OK to never pray at all for anything but for help. A "thanks" afterward is good, but not mandatory. There's no magic quota of one type of prayer needed to offset another type of prayer. If you never prayed for anything in your whole life except for help, that is just fine. Remember… no rules.

Pray for help to figure out what is making you unhappy. I don't like acronyms (words formed from the initials of several words) because I never can think of them when I need them, but I do use one regularly to check in on my feelings: **H-A-L-T**. I ask myself, am I ***Hungry, Angry, Lonely, or Tired***? These four feelings come up regularly in all of us. It's powerful to know what's bothering you. Name the demon, so to speak. At least you know what to pray for.

Sometimes you don't need to pray; you just need to eat.

We pray for help to resist a temptation. (I can resist anything but temptation.)

We pray for help to remove a particular character defect or a bad habit (a "thorn in your flesh"). Maybe God wants you to live with that "thorn" as part of your spiritual path. Or, maybe He uses you, and your "problem," to affect someone else's life in some way.

Pray for help to have the patience to just see what happens. It's a relief to know you don't have to be in charge. These can be prayers of surrender. "I give up. You take it."

A please help prayer will not always be answered immediately with a solution. God has his own way with time. We don't know if time for Him is all right now, or all eternity. You may send prayers and not get answers until later, sometimes much later. Sometimes no answer is an answer. Time is a problem for us, but is not the slightest problem for God.

Prayers you send out may conflict with others' prayers. Sometimes just ask to be led, knowing that you don't have the big picture. None of us has an idea of the overall plan for our own lives, much less the lives of others. Ask for a "win-win." I have never had a day without surprises and changes in plans.

All species cry out in fear and panic. Sometimes we cry prayers for help with groans, cries, or screams like animals that can't talk, when words cannot express how we feel.

When we are confronted with anguish, misery, pain, loss, or sickness, sometimes we feel we must pray. In the immediacy of it all, just let it flow.

As psychobiologist Joan Borysenko states in her book *Guilt Is the Teacher, Love Is the Lesson*[2]:

*When we are absolutely miserable, prayer is no longer a dry rote repetition.*

---

2   Guilt Is The Teacher; Love Is The Lesson, HayHouse.com, Joan Borysenko PhD.

*It becomes a living and vibrant cry for help. It becomes authentic. In pain we forget the "thee's" and "thou's" that keep us separated from God, and reach a new state of intimacy that comes from talking to God in our own way, saying what is in our heart.*

**PRAYER TIP #2: When things are really bad, start with a "Please Help," then just do a "stream of consciousness" whine or babble, out loud, in a whisper, or just think it. God's listening. You don't have to compose a prayer. Just do a prayer. Cry a prayer. Sob a prayer.**

## PRAYING FOR FORGIVENESS:
God is really big on forgiveness. All His religions have forgiveness as an integral part.

We all make mistakes. Say things we wish we hadn't. Do things we regret. We wish we could have "do-overs." A prayer asking for forgiveness is kind of a confession. (Half the steps in the Alcoholic Anonymous Twelve Step program are confessional.) If you confess to yourself and God, it means you clearly intend to deal with your faults and temptations.

God knows you need to let go of the past. God's not in the past. But, He can help you change your version of the past. Forgiveness is not letting the past run or ruin the present. It's OK to glimpse back at the past, but not to live there.

Wrongs against you can afflict you with suffering. They're like curses because you keep them simmering. It is your baggage. Sometimes the only way to make those curses powerless is by forgiving those who caused them. They don't need to know you have forgiven them. They may not even know they need forgiveness. What they did may not have been mean and intentional. You just think it was. You took it personally. You made assumptions. But maybe it's you that needs to release the curse.

"Pack your bags, you're going on a guilt trip."

Unpack your bags.

It is *your* baggage that you need to drop. Extra baggage always costs you. Even the airlines charge for it.

It is not easy, or pleasant, doing "forgiveness-work." But it has to be done, or you will continue to suffer from your miserable anger. Ever hold a grudge? Whatever they did to you, they most likely don't remember, or care. You're the one remembering. God's not in the past. Let go of that grudge. (I have a drawer full of medals for *Holding-a-Grudge*.)

Here's how I do "forgiveness-work." It's not always 100 percent effective, but it gets easier and quicker with practice.

First, I ask for help: *Help me completely forgive _____, and the whole business in question.*

Second, I give God his due: *You're great to take this awful burden from me. You know best what to do with it.*

Thirdly, I thank God: *Thanks for setting both of us free.*"

It's just another *Please help; Thanks; God you're great* prayer, isn't it?

Then, whenever the memory of the offense happens to come to mind, I repeat the prayer and ask God to take it again.

Additionally, I try to, sometime during every day, issue a *general amnesty* prayer, forgiving everybody who has ever done me wrong. One trick I use to remind myself to do my forgiveness work is when I see the color puce-green; I say my general amnesty prayer. (For some reason I detest that color. Maybe it reminds me of the Army.) The other day, I saw the color puce on two ladies in the same parking lot at the same time. God must have been serious about me doing my forgiveness work that day!

By the way, just because you've forgiven somebody, that doesn't mean you are compelled to like that person. You can do an *I-can't-stand-you prayer*: "I can't stand this person, but I wish them well just the same. Take my worst enemy, God, and smite him!" (Well, OK, maybe leave off the smite thing—that's not exactly wishing them well. Besides He might smite you; maybe you are your own worst enemy.) I don't have to like everybody. Neither do you.

Use a forgiveness prayer even as something is happening that is "unforgivable." (Think of the baggage you wouldn't even have to claim.) Give an instant forgiveness prayer a name, like the *Black*

*Prayer*, and have it ready to fire from the hip. *"This jerk doesn't know what he's doing. Help me not be affected by him. Thanks. You're great."* (Smite him!) What they are putting out there to affect you negatively will come back at them. That person isn't going to get along well in the world acting like a jerk. Maybe God is teaching a lesson—that person will get his way more often if he doesn't behave like a jerk— and you are just part of one of God's plans. Play along.

Then there's the Lord's Prayer: "Forgive us our trespasses as we forgive those that trespass against us." We can't demand our own forgiveness…without releasing others as well.

One thing for sure; I'm not supposed to be a judge and censor for others' actions. Judging is best left to God. If I don't judge, then I don't even have to forgive.

## PRAYING FOR OTHERS:
Those in need, sickness, life-threatening situations, etc., need all the prayer they can get. Everybody can use a good "praying-for" from time to time.

Pray for help, whatever the problem is, and thank God for looking into it, and praise Him for his power to help. *Please help; thanks; You're great:*

*Please help _____ have the strength to get through this.*

*Thank You for giving this matter Your attention God. Only You can know what to do. I leave it all in Your hands.*

*You're the greatest.*

You don't have to stop what you are doing and compose it. Keep it short and simple. As the image of someone who needs help pops into your head, say a prayer for them. Or just think it.

I sometimes use what I call the RICOCHET prayer to pray for others. This is a thought, or spoken prayer that I send straight up to God in heaven (think communication satellite), and it bounces back down to whomever I want to receive it. It bounces off God. This is particularly useful for sending prayers across town, to another city, or even to the other side of the world.

I call another one the SATURATION prayer. I imagine radiation coming out of my hands and eyes that contain love, hope, and care. I direct these thoughts toward someone and saturate them with prayer. Sometimes it goes on for several minutes, almost a meditation all about them. Other times it is a "quickie." The person may be in trouble, pain, or danger; or be getting ready for a trip, marriage, or a new job. Or just a jerk in his way. Sometimes I can see the worry, or fear, on their face. Maybe they told me of an issue or problem. Sometimes I ask them if I can pray for them and even direct my palms toward them. Most times, I just do it silently, anonymously.

I randomly pray for strangers. One method I use

I call the LEFTTURN-SANCTION; I'm stopped at a red light. The left turn arrow is on for people turning left from my right, and they are passing in front of me. I look at their faces. They all look intent on what they are doing. They look likable. I could see them as a friend. As they sweep in front of me, one by one, I wish them well, or bless them. "God bless that one… and that one… and that one…."

Be careful. When you pray for someone it may be for them to change. But people are stubbornly not changeable. Be careful that your prayers for others are not just really saying, why can't you be more like me? Sometimes your prayers are coming from your need to control them and are judgmental in nature. You may be passing judgment. But judgment is for God. (I have a black belt in *Manage-Manipulate-and-Control*.)

It can be an uncomfortable struggle, and painful, when we open ourselves to the will of God, and invite him to change whatever needs changing, and find out it's us, and not another that needs changing.

There are times that you know someone is doing the wrong thing. They may even know they're doing the wrong thing. And you want to save them; *rescue them*. Maybe they are repeating the same mistake they've made before.

Prayer for others might be wrestling with God for control. "Why don't they do what I want? I know I'm right. Why are they so stubborn?" Maybe they're in the middle of a lesson, and you need to get out of the way, and let them learn it. (Or, maybe God is using them to teach you a lesson.) Do you ever know the whole story in someone's life? There is always more information. There are circumstances you don't know about. Even with your loved ones and close friends.

God has a higher vision of individuals than they have of themselves. We are apologetic about our shortcomings. We discount our talents and good features. We compare ourselves constantly to those that we see as better. We're pretty hard on ourselves. Give someone a boost with the following prayer. This is maybe the greatest prayer blessing you can say to someone:

*"Let me tell you something. If you haven't heard this before, I consider it a privilege to be the one to tell you this...."* At this point tell them all the good feelings and observations you have about them. Watch the magic! Come to someone without judgment and threat, with a positive attitude, and you'll get the same in return. And it makes you feel good. (It's all about me.)

As with any prayer, but especially when praying for others, it's easy to blame ourselves for prayer-failure. We didn't pray it right, or hard enough, or long enough. We didn't say the right words. We are unworthy to ask for God's help. We may even see it as our lack of faith, even though the request was made with weighty faith. Don't ever feel that something didn't happen because there is something wrong with your praying skills. God is the one in control. And His ways are not always known, or revealed.

Be careful with this praying for others in another way. There are so many that need prayer... but it's not possible to do every good work that needs to be done. It does not all depend on you. Don't make your "prayer-list" impossibly long.

**PRAYER FOR HELP TO LET GO:**
We tend to see many circumstances as too complicated and serious. We torture ourselves over decisions about situation after situation, convinced that every facet of our lives is crucially vital to our survival. Sometimes we're just way too frantic. The truth is you don't have to live a focused, determined, purposeful life *all the time*. You don't *always* have to be productive. Struggle and process are not always necessary. You don't always have to do your best.

Ask for help "letting go" of some of that intensity and craziness.

There are unhappy things that happen to us every day that we have zero power over (unseen cosmic-two-by-fours whacking us on the back of the head). Many aren't our fault. It's just life as humans, here, on the frantic planet. Of course, some are our own fault because we are willful, selfish, and deceitful children sometimes. We can be obstinate, insensitive, and prejudiced. No one can create messes for us like ourselves. (I could get a six-foot trophy for: "*Messing-Up-My-Life*.")

We obsessively analyze every fearful emotion. We think the job of living is huge, and that failure and disaster are always near, and others are always ready to hurt us, or take our share.

We repress uncomfortable thoughts into inaccessible areas of our mind.

We know how to "suffer well." Everyone has a good crisis story. Everyone has a better suffering story than you.

We love to have something to fix about ourselves. We can even make it our life's work: the *addiction to transformation*; the *infection of perfection.* We're addicted to our roller coaster.

We want perfection from everyone in all circumstances, including ourselves. Except we all define perfection differently, so up pops control issues. Or we have our own agenda and priorities.

We all have our own perspective. No situation looks exactly the same to two observers. Ask a cop taking statements at the scene of an accident. Witnesses rarely report the same observations. (And they may change their account later.)

We blow up even the simplest concerns. Sometimes a new problem in another area of our tortured existence forces us to abandon our attention on the current *worry-of-the-hour* (maybe allowing the crisis to resolve itself). We sometimes forget problems only because we swap them with others.

Every fight seems justified.

It is important to be right.

We might even have had pounded into us that *not winning* is a sign of *weakness*.

Stop "catching" someone's attacks. Learn to duck instead, and let them just zing on by. Don't catch an "anger-ball," and then throw it back. Say a prayer for help not to catch it in the first place.

We repeatedly find ourselves at odds with other willful humans. They're thinking only of themselves too. *Willfulness* is in our nature. In fact, God gave us "free-will." We can behave like willful children. (What grade are you in today?)

Do you need help letting go of the tendency to take to heart everything hurtful coming your way? Are you the star of a soap-drama, or a sit-com? That you are writing?

Do yourself a favor; release the need to control others or your circumstances. (You want to hear God laugh? Tell Him your plans.)

Wouldn't it be nice to have some help dealing with other people? So, ask for it. Let them go. Let God deal with jerks. (He must love jerks—there are a lot of them!) You're just one small human (jerk)… you can't be expected to be able to change all the jerks in the world. Besides the problem with others is never about what it looks like; you never have the whole story.

Letting go… and letting God deal with stuff… is a good reason "why" to pray. No one thinks you can do everything on your own all the time anyway. Especially God. Pain is always due to resisting and not letting go. Ask for the wisdom to choose the path of least resistance.

Be careful. Sometimes when you let go of something it leaves a vacuum. Be ready to fill that space with something good. It may be an ice cream cone, or a movie, or a call to a friend, telling them what you let go of.

***PRAYER TIP #3: Pray to just let it go—seek no answer, seek no solution, and seek no results. Remember you can choose after you choose, if what you chose isn't working. Give it to God. Let go; let God. Take away its power on you and it will fade into nothingness.***

## PRAYER FOR HELP WITH OUR RELATIONSHIPS:

We got our life-skills training from parents, friends, teachers, coaches, etc. They may not have been all that good with life skills. We learn to deceive, and explore in hiding, since others (parents and lovers) may not want us to explore with wonder. We are hung up on who we think we are. We act who we think we are so much we don't feel right about who we really are.

We may have been taught how to love by others who didn't know how to love. We may love the wrong things. We may love the wrong way. We may love for the wrong reasons. We may love because we are told we *have* to.

We may even have been taught that being altruistic, charitable, loving, spiritual, and forgiving were signs of weakness, or being irresponsible.

Conflict in relationships is often friction between two fictions.

Our relationships usually begin with dishonesty. We enhance our achievements, and cover up, or discount, our flaws. We shift the blame for our failures to others. Or we lie-by-omission; we just don't talk about our dark parts. As we progress into the relationship, we may not admit or tolerate our own imperfections, so we can't tolerate imperfections in anyone else. Relationships are rarely a smooth road. They are more like a minefield. As the relationship continues these imperfections start surfacing.

Finally, we walk away from those relationships that become unpleasant only to enter another just as hostile. It sometimes is the adversarial relationship that teaches us the most. We grow by facing our faults. Sometimes we didn't know we had them until someone pointed them out.

Relationships are rich breeding grounds for please-help prayers. If you forget to pray, someone is going to come along and remind you. (My kids used to just love to make me pray... *"We're here to push every button you've got."*)

People sometimes push your buttons to remind you they are there. OK, fine. So, pray for them instead of pushing back. Maybe God's pushing you, through them.

We can really shine at pushing the buttons of others; the "shame-and-blame" buttons particularly. We try to get everyone to change according to our specifications. We find it irresistible not to send people on a "guilt trip." But they can be defiant. (*Shame-and-Blame?* I could get a trophy for that too.)

Interestingly, and repeatedly, if you accept them as they are, they change, in spite of you (or to spite you?). Besides maybe they're being taught a lesson, so maybe you should let them learn it and get out of the way. (Let go, let God.) Like: "I told her she should be a nurse. We split up, and she went to nursing school."

Isn't it interesting that it's often our loved ones that we assail the most, because they are safe to attack? We know they will still love us anyway. (Of course, they attack you for all the same reasons you attack them.)

Sometimes we start arguments as a way of diverting attention away from ourselves, and our painful inadequacies (real or made up?). And those miserable souls we direct our frustrations to, counter-attack of course.

With a little prayer, maybe we can discover that we all don't need to get along delightfully and agreeably all the time. The relationship doesn't have to be blissful minute by minute to be successful. Maybe we aren't right all the time.

(Note: This is not a book about relationships. If you want to know if you are in a "toxic" relationship, see Appendix One. Each point may describe part of your situation. It helps sometimes to name the problem. Then you know what to pray for.)

***PRAYER TIP #4:** Try not being **JUDGMENTAL** for one day. Imagine those you are about to judge bathed in light, and you're bathed in light too. Ask God to merge the two lights. "Please help me, God, not be judgmental, and see the light. Thanks."*

## PRAYER FOR HELP WITH OUR FEELING OF LACK; NOT HAVING ENOUGH:

We're not getting our piece of the pie. We feel sorry for ourselves. There's never enough money. We compare ourselves to the Jones' relentlessly and obsessively; they have more, and that's not fair. Slice me up and everybody pour salt on it. You feel like the last brick laid, and the first brick stepped on.

Deep down inside, we may feel like we deserve lack, like we have brought it upon ourselves. And not just the lack of material things; we may feel we are not worthy of the love we crave from others, especially if they knew about the "real" us.

A lot of us are lack driven; the glass is half-empty, not half-full. We are failures in getting our share. There is only so much "pie" and we have to fight for our piece. We want extra pie in a safe. We want some of your pie too. There isn't enough pie for all of us. We want what you have, and resent you for having it.

Imagine if we had a choice to breathe or not to breathe. What would you hear humans say?

I want some of *your* breath.
I will take extra breaths and *store* them.
You *don't deserve* any breaths.
I'm *not worthy*, so I won't breathe.

We fear failure. We were taught the dreadful message of equating our self-worth with our failures. (From those flawed teachers from our youth again?) And with fear of failure comes fear of lack. It's about competition for pieces of the pie.

If only I had found the right clothes, school, job, friends, lover. If only I had enough money, that car, that house, that body.

Everybody told you growing up, "Just do your best." Do you always do your best? The best job possible with everything you do? It is the illusion that perfection is possible. And if this and that isn't perfect, then you lack something. *Achievement neurosis*: the value of your selfworth is the amount of success or stuff you have. All outside of you.

What's wrong with an average day? An average meal? An average walk in the park? An average bicycle ride? It's way easier to be content with yourself if you don't make impossible demands on yourself.

God can be perfect, but we don't have to apply that standard to ourselves.

How about maybe you don't always do your best. Maybe start right now by trying an average prayer.

*Please help me God not to be too worried about doing my best, and stop blaming myself all the time for*

*all the stuff I think I lack;*
　*Thanks for the stuff I have;*
　*You're the greatest.*

**PRAYER FOR HELP WITH ANGER:**
When we're angry we can get ourselves in trouble with our mouth, or our behavior. Whether you scream, sulk in cold silence, lash out with cruel words, or even act out physically, anger is devastating to your happiness. Prayer may be the only way to control it.

God works with you when you're angry. If you're **H-O-T** you're: *Honest*, *Open*, and *Transparent*. (There's one of those stupid acronyms again. Forget it.) When the heat of the moment has passed, we often feel the need to pray. Really good prayer can be *emotion remembered in tranquility*.

Of course, it's ideal not to get angry in the first place. Pray for it not to even come. Or if you get angry, pray that anger away before it really catches fire, and explodes. Anger is bad for you. It causes ulcers, insomnia, fatigue; it messes up relationships; it leads to guilt and depression; it's embarrassing. And it's like throwing a glass of water over a waterfall; it doesn't make any difference. It never changes things. It doesn't work to get you what you want. In fact, it usually gets the opposite of what you want. Whoever you are raging at doesn't change, but they want to change you to get you under control. (Or if he's your waiter, he spits in your food.)

It can become a bad habit. It's an over-kill way to handle frustration.

Fifty percent of what you believe will be disapproved of, or disagreed with, by fifty percent of the population, fifty percent of the time. You're going to get 150-percent frustrated. That's going to make you angry. One-hundred-percent guaranteed.

Your way is not the only way. God gave us all free will to think up all those different perspectives. People are just going to "free-will" all over you.

This is not a self-help book, or a psychology text. It's about how easy it is to pray. Anger, if nothing else, will get you closer to God, because the only way out of it sometimes is to pray it away. Maybe you're angry because God wants to get your attention. He's working on you by making you angry.

At least while you're asking God for help, you are diffusing, or weakening your anger and rage. Rage rarely lasts very long. Ever try to pray and be angry at the same time. By the time the prayer is over, the heat of the moment will be starting to cool. Thomas Jefferson said, "When angry, count ten before you speak; if very angry, a hundred." Counting to ten is just a prayer for patience, or for help to not make a fool out of yourself.

Ask God to help you remember that the person in your face is just another one of His jerks. He sends them your way all the time. (Like I said, He must really love jerks.)

Also, ask God to remind you that you've probably done exactly the same thing to someone.

(Driving is endlessly full of opportunities to touch base with God.)

You are pretty much powerless over people. Very little of what they do can be controlled by you. We are all willful children, trying to snatch our piece of the pie. Anger may give you an illusion of power, but the object of your anger may just be appeasing you to placate you, and they can't wait to pay you back.

Like I said, it's best to just do nothing. Just sit there… and think up a prayer:

*Thank you for guiding my hands on the steering wheel, and my foot on the brake.*

*Protect that jerk that cut me off and thank you for not letting me road rage.*

*You're the greatest, and thanks for saving us both.*

A lot of what happens to us is a direct result of what we send out from ourselves. Cliché time: *What goes around, comes around…. You reap what you sew…. Thoughts in mind, create like kind.* An angry person can walk into a room and you can tell they're angry even if they don't say anything. Anger is contagious… everyone picks up on it. Maybe they zing an "angerball" at you; you catch it and launch it right back at them, or at someone else, like a shortstop catching a line drive in baseball. Maybe it wasn't even words, just a smug, or haughty dirty look, so you stare one back. You know, stick your tongue out at them like a little kid. Maybe you're the angry person walking into the room? Well, it is 100 percent guaranteed that you will get anger back.

Sometimes people verbally attack; the snide remark, ridicule, holier-than-thou patronizing, sanctimonious, passive-aggressive... whatever. So, you say something equally unpleasant in return. You almost can't help it. They put it out there. They started it. What do they expect?

Go ahead and acknowledge your evil thoughts and feelings, but then ask God for some help "building a bridge." (So, you can "get over it.")

Here's an example:

*"Lord, please keep telling me that this too will pass. I thank you, God, that I don't have to live with this miserable human being. Help me build a bridge so I can get over it."*

Or... maybe you actually have to live with a miserable human being (a real sociopathic jerk). Turn bad thoughts into a good prayer:

*God, please stop me from choking him with my bare hands the next time I see him, for not filling the car after he used it, and not answering his cell phone. Please make him answer so I can inform him heatedly to bring me a can of gas now that I'm stranded, and give him hell for causing this mess in the first place, by stupidly feeding the turkey bones to the dog, who is vomiting in the back seat of this out-of-gas car. At least my jerk son is making me talk to You, God. Thanks, and again, please help."*

All of us can be willful, selfish, petty, inconsiderate, and childish. Who hasn't had a bad day because of another human?

*"Oh, God, help me not allow another's bad day create one in me too. Help him see how petty, inconsiderate, selfish, and childish he is, even if he is my husband. Help me let go of my intense desire to harm him. I'm begging here. You're the Greatest. Thanks."*

That prayer has it all. "Help me, help him, give me, let go, You're great, and thank You!" See, praying is simple. Just talk normal.

***PRAYER TIP #5: What if you do catch the anger-ball? Throw it back at God instead of whoever threw it at you. God's safe. You can't do anything to make God stop loving you.***

## PRAYER FOR THANKS:
There is always something to thank God for:

Thank God for solving your problems from yesterday. He wants you to learn from the past, not protest or complain about it today. Most everything you're worried about today will be history tomorrow, and replaced by your next set of worries anyway. You might as well forget them today as tomorrow. (Remember, God's everywhere but in the past.)

How about thanking God for the skillful repair jobs to your body that you have so sloppily abused? Like, "thanks for survival thus far."

How about thanks for air, food, and water.

How about the wealth of experience you've accumulated? "Been there; done that; don't have to do that again."

I use the alphabet sometimes. I think of something I'm grateful for, for each letter. A-apples; B-bathrooms; C-candy; D-dogs; E-eating; F-friends; G-God...

Here's a good "thanks" prayer:

*I am not the person I want to be;*
*I am not the person I ought to be;*
*Thank God I'm not the person I used to be.*

You may just have to fake gratitude. Inside you may actually be a willful, deceitful child, all about your dark parts, and trying to take everyone else's piece of pie. Fake gratitude? There are catchy little phrases that can help: "fake it till you make it!" "An attitude of gratitude." Even if you don't feel particularly grateful—fake it. Your brain actually changes with practice, as if you were practicing a musical instrument.

Sometimes that's why prayer works; it changes you. If you feel thankful, maybe you won't be such a jerk always wanting someone else's piece of pie. So, people might like you better. Then maybe you'll be happier. Prayer can be faking it until you make it.

By the way, when you say a thank-you prayer in front of people, it makes you sound like a wonderful person; altruistic, loving, spiritual, and forgiving. That can be rather impressive to mothers-in-law, the scoutmaster, the church small group, and bosses.

Offers of thanks can be forced on us when we are asked to say a prayer out loud. Like the fearsome and dreaded; "Would you say grace?"

The three-part prayer is perfect for this:

*Thank You for providing this food. (bounty, abundance, etc.)*

*You're the greatest.*

*Please help us put it to good use by sharing with others.*

You may be thinking another prayer:

*Help me not get food poisoning from my mother-in-law's cooking.*

*(Again.)*

*Thank God this is only once a year.*

*Help me find some Pepto-Bismol.*

(Stupid, I know. Thank God I have a forgiving God, with a sense of humor.)

A theologian, Meister Eckhart, from a long time ago said, "If the only prayer you said in your whole life was, 'thank you,' that would suffice."

I say, a really bad moment for an atheist is when he is really grateful, and has nobody to thank.

## PRAYER FOR A REALITY CHECK:
Denial is the refusal to accept reality because it is too threatening.

Minimization is reality diluted.

Rationalization can be actually a way of justifying your unacceptable actions with excuses.

We disguise a weakness by emphasizing a strength.

We fantasize to escape reality.

We displace our own shame onto others. We blame others for our shortcomings.

These defense mechanisms often occur unconsciously. They tend to distort, transform, or otherwise falsify, reality. They hinder us from being creative, self-sufficient, authentic, playful, accepting of others, appreciative, and spontaneous. Altered reality prevents the uncovering of painful aspects of life that we need to deal with to grow up. We need real reality.

Am I doing the right thing? Is this the right choice? Even at the busiest time of the day, I take moments to check in with God; *especially* if I'm really busy.

I try to never be so convinced of something that I can't look at new evidence.

When I come to decision time, I ask God what I should do. Or if what I am going to do is the right thing. I often get an answer immediately. It's amazing.

Sometimes I don't get an answer immediately. That can actually be an answer. It may mean I'm not ready for an answer; that I need to put it on the back burner, and ask again in a while. Or sleep on it. "No answer" can mean "have patience."

I always ask for guidance when I'm thinking about buying something. I'm not talking choosing a brand of milk, or a lottery ticket. I'm talking a Mercedes. I pray to remember the old fairytale that material things bring happiness. *Reality:* is it going to make me just as happy as the last time I thought buying something would make me happy? (It didn't make me happy.)

I'm not saying luxury is wrong. I'm not saying something expensive is a bad idea. The same God that made Ford Pintos, makes Mercedes. Put it out there. If you want a Mercedes, put it out there. Ask the universe. Ask for abundance. I love the saying: *Thoughts in mind create like kind.* Nothing happens unless you start the ball rolling. All things begin with you creating a thought.

The answer is always NO, if you don't ask for something.

I'm just saying you may not be coming from a position of reality when it comes to this moment in time... particularly when you are buying something and hoping for the answer to the meaning of life.

A great time to pray is when you're about to buy something. Ask for a reality check.

*All faiths are welcomed. Or none. We plan a special edition* **PRAYER LITE** *for different religious paths.*

# CHAPTER FOUR

### PRAYER WORKS

In the now-classic study performed by cardiologist Randolph Byrd[3], 393 patients that were admitted to the coronary-care unit at San Francisco General Hospital, were randomly assigned to either a group that was prayed for by home-prayer groups, or a group that was not prayed for. There were 192 patients in the prayed-for group; and 201 in the not-prayed-for group.

The prayed-for group:

- Were five times less likely to require antibiotics.
- Three times less likely to develop pulmonary edema. (This is a condition where the lungs fill with fluid due to changes in pressure throughout

---

[3] Southern Medical Journal, December, 1988, Randolph Byrd MD.

the circulatory system as a consequence of the heart failing to pump blood properly.)
- None required endotracheal intubation and attachment to a mechanical ventilator.
- Fewer in the prayed-for group died.

In an emergency room on a Sunday night at a busy hospital, I was immersed in my personal drama. The staff was worn out, cranky, snapping at each other, overwhelmed. The nasty energy in the room was palatable—you could taste the touchy, exasperated, bitterness frustration—even anger.

Everybody was thinking, "Why me?"

I was irritated with every one of the staff for not treating me like I was the only one there. (It's all about me.)

The dirty, snotty, whiny, fidgety kids (mine), and their dirty, raggedy, fidgety parent (me); the stupid sick-stuff smells; the noise pollution (stupid elevator music); and the visual pollution (stupid dusty fake potted plants) … I was cranked up.

I said to myself, *it's time to pray*.

My first prayer probably wasn't a prayer; more of a blasphemy.

Then I started praying for serenity and strength for each worker, one at a time. I spent maybe thirty seconds or so, looking and focusing on each nurse, orderly, doctor, and aide, one at a time. It took all of maybe ten minutes to pray for all of them. I wasn't doing anything anyway except getting more and more freaky myself.

Here's what I said as best as I can remember: As I intently stared at each one with my full undivided attention (they didn't know it—that would have been creepy) I said to myself, *Please, God, give this poor, tired, overworked, good person a little boost of energy and patience, and help him/her look out for his/her fellow workers. Thanks. You're great.*

After I prayed individually for each of them, I just sat there and thought about that individual in a nice way. I tried to find some nice feature about each one. I thought about what they must be feeling or thinking. What their family might be like. And I thanked God for having them here to take care of me (it's all about me.) That's it. Then I went on to the next one.

Confusion began to ease up. Some "shift" happened. They softened. Their voices weren't as shrill. They quit throwing clip boards down noisily; slamming doors. Dirty looks stopped.

It was the first time I had ever tried that and it worked! I was astounded.

Everyone in the whole ER got nicer sort of all of a sudden. Children quit screeching. Conversations got muted, as opposed to shrill. I couldn't believe it. It spread.

Simply pray. Prayer simply works. I believe it now.

You can turn *bad thoughts* into *good prayers*. You can start your day over anytime you choose.

Prayer works for me.

It's been said that the only scoffers of prayer are those who never tried it enough.

I want to be serene. I want to feel comfortable with my place in the world. If that's all I ever get from prayer, that's enough to prove to me it works.

Lonely? Prayer reminds me that I am not alone. That works for me.

Anxious? Desperate? I pray to let go, and land in a safety net. That works for me.

With regular prayer, you'll be more loving, kind, gentle, considerate, and forgiving; treat others as equals; catch a glimpse of God in everyone; and be surprisingly free of anxiety. That works for me.

I don't have to pretend I'm someone I'm not when I pray. That works for me.

I can let people be as they're meant to be, and that removes a huge burden from my shoulders from trying to control them and outcomes. That works for me.

Prayer makes me happier. It works for me. (It's all about me.)

Prayer works.

# CHAPTER FIVE

**HOW TO PRAY OUT LOUD—EVEN WHEN YOU'RE SHY.**

Are you a ***Prayer-a-phobe***? Are you terrified of being asked to pray in public? You're in good company. Maybe that's why someone asks you to say the prayer; they don't want to. Or they're testing you, just as you feared.

Someday you'll be called upon to give an ***OUT OF THE BLUE PRAYER*** whether you're ready or not.

We have all been cornered:

- Holiday dinner; out of the blue, your mother-in-law asks you to say grace. (Last thanksgiving your self-righteous, smug, successful, and wealthy, handsome, brother-in-law, effortlessly spewed one out that was so good the women cried.)

- The scoutmaster asks you to say a "little prayer" in front of the kids and leaders. Last troop meeting an eleven-year-old (just back from bible camp) fluidly sent one to heaven like a TV evangelist. (When I went to bible camp all I learned was smoking.)
- Or the church "small group" you just joined wants you to start the evening with a prayer, all holding hands, heads bowed. (At least they can't see the panic and horror in your eyes. The real reason you joined the group is holding your suddenly clammy hand.)
- Or your boss (The Deacon) asks you to kick off the business meeting with a little prayer. (You're not sure what a deacon is.)

You can do it! It's stupid easy. Anyone can do it, no matter how shy you are. Remember, prayer is simple: three parts; in any order.

Just think:

1. **Please Help.**
2. **God, You're great.** (Powerful, loving, awesome, caring…etc.)
3. **Thanks.**

EXAMPLES:
- At the dinner table with mother in law: "**Thanks** for the excellent food. **You're great** to give this to us, God. **Help** us use it for Your good."

Prayer Lite

- At the scout meeting: "**Thanks** for all these kids and parents. **You're awesome** to give us this time together. **Help** us all do good as a group.
- In the hospital: "**Help** ____ to ____. **Thanks** for being with us, **merciful Father**. May Your will be done."
- To launch the sales meeting: "**Thanks** for the opportunity to share time together. **You're wonderful** to give this to us. **Help** us as a group, and individually, to do good for all of us here, and our company." (God likes to be your business partner, by the way.)

***PRAYER TIP # 6: <u>Asked to say a prayer in front of a group</u>? And you actually really are shy? You don't even have to say it a prayer... just ask for a "moment of silence." Or you can take a moment of silence to get your act together, to think about what to say. Then a "Please" and a "Thanks" and a "God is great." That's all you need. Taking a moment of silence lets the others center themselves a little too."***

Here are some <u>specific ideas</u> on how to be ready in case you are asked to say an out-of-the-blue prayer:

- Don't leave home without a prayer in mind. Have something to say already cooked up relating to what you're going to be doing, just in case you get called on. It's less of a struggle to think up a prayer at your desk, or in the car, then thinking one up on your feet, in front of a crowd. (Thinking of a prayer before needing a prayer is praying, by the way, in case you don't want to go where you're going and need help not being a jerk when you get there.)

- Try not hiding your shyness. People sometimes think shyness is aloofness, arrogance, being stuck up, or that you don't like them. But if you announce that you're nervous in front of the others, you'll have instant understanding and support from those around you.
- Sometimes it's good to have multiple things to be thankful for. You can pad a prayer easily making it longer by adding additional "thank-you's." They're easy to think of: food, water, air, life, shelter, friends, opportunity… Or you can randomly pick a letter of the alphabet then think of a word that letter begins with; F-fellowship, L-love, P-peace, S-serenity, M-money….
- Turn it around. Put someone else in the spotlight. Ask individuals in the group what they would like you to pray for. Sometimes there's someone who just can't wait to make it easy for you. (Fifty percent of the world is shy too, so you may not get anything out of them.)
- You don't have to be an expert with a guitar to be able to play "Boléro." You can learn one guitar piece. Get one good prayer memorized.

Those really good sounding TV evangelists have dozens of prayer parts memorized, and although they sound like they are making a prayer up from scratch, they are often just stringing together memorized phrases. They know the language. Memorize a few "prayer-sentences" of your own so you can appear fluent in prayer-ese too.

- Close your eyes and visualize for a few seconds before you open your mouth. God will come to your rescue. Maybe picture yourself sitting on God's lap like a child on a parent's lap. Open your eyes and look up (with your best pleading look), like you're looking at God Himself (this buys time to think), and then start with the thanks part first (it's the easiest). *"Thanks, God, for hearing my prayer.... Thanks, God, for being with us today.... Thanks, God, for the food.... Thanks, God, for all these friends...."* Always have a couple of "Thanks, God" phrases ready. They are good while you are trying to think up what you really want to say. Then do your *Please help*, and *God is great* parts.

- Use a prayer you've already memorized, like; *"Bless this food to our use, and us to Thy service."* Or start your prayer the same as the Lord's Prayer: *"Our Father, Who art in Heaven...* then add a *"Please Help us."* Or, you can borrow one of this author's personal memorized favorites: *"Good food, good meat, good God, let's eat! Praise the Lord. And all the brothers and sisters*

*say, Amen!"* (God loves it when His children laugh. Remember; no rules.)
- Tell God *where* you are. That's always a good way to get started. *"We are gathered here together.... Hear our prayer as we stand beside this hospital bed.... As we get on this airplane, we ask.... As we draw together for this meeting with friends and colleagues, we ask.... As I walk down the aisle, help me not run...."*

***PRAYER TIP #8: Be prepared. Don't leave home without a prayer if you think there is even a remote chance you'll be asked to say one. You can just start any prayer with "We are gathered here together to…." Then remember the three parts: 1. Please… 2. Thanks… 3. some version of "God, You're great."***

If the whole group is shy; try a **SPIRITUAL CAR WASH**:

Don't even say a prayer. Do a prayer.

Line everyone up shoulder to shoulder. Line up like cars in line at the car wash. One by one, the last person in the line, starts from his or her end of the line, and works their way down the line facing each person one at a time and prays for them. Like the different segments of a carwash.

These prayers can also be "touch prayers," said with a light touch on the shoulder, or holding hands. Many people don't like to be touched, but in the right circumstances it's fine.

# CHAPTER SIX

**MEDITATION: INQUIRE WITHIN!**

**MEDITATION** (Encarta Dictionary): The emptying of the mind of thoughts, or the concentration of the mind on one thing, in order to aid mental or spiritual development, contemplation, or relaxation.

In all religions and cultures, "going within" is considered pivotal to being intimate with God. We talk too much. We think too much. We worry too much. The constant chatter in our minds, some call "monkey talk." Meditation is a way to clear the mind of that static so you can listen to God.

It would be easy to be contemplative on a mountain top, or in a monastery. We would probably be pretty good at connecting with God if we spent a year in a cave burning incense sticks, watching the seasons pass, and beating on a drum.

But God gave us jobs, relationships, kids, responsibilities. And only so much time. And we keep piling it on. If we're not living on the edge, we're taking up too much room. Then there's a football game that needs watching.

You don't have to meditate for long. Five or ten minutes is plenty. Leave for work fifteen minutes early and park in an empty church lot. Sit outside for twenty minutes during lunch. Five or ten minutes before bed.

Meditation clears your mind so you can listen to God. He'll get your attention one way or another. Like parenting, first you try nice and quiet, but if the children don't listen, you notch it up. God will do the same; nice and quiet at first. If you're not paying attention, He'll notch it up. He'll use a "cosmic-two-by-four" to get your attention if he has to. Then maybe you'll listen. Meditation is easier… and it's nice and quiet.

Meditation helps you make better decisions from a good place of serenity and clear headedness, instead of in the heat of the moment. How did those decisions turn out when you were red-faced?

Meditation is opening to God, not talking to God. He does the talking, not you. This is really easy prayer.

Meditation makes you healthier, less anxious, less defensive, and helps you de-stress. Stress affects everything in your body; your heart, digestive tract, endocrine system, immune system, etc.

The results of meditation have been compared to REM sleep. Among other things, meditation and REM sleep both prevent the release of neurotransmitters that make you edgy and jagged, like norepinephrine, serotonin, and histamine. These hormones are sometimes referred to as "stress hormones" and needed for the "fight-or-flight" responses of your body, by increasing the heart rate, releasing glucose and cortisol into the bloodstream, etc. It is also believed that REM sleep and meditation stimulate "associative networks" in the brain helping it make connections of different unrelated ideas. This enhances problem-solving, decision-making, and increases creativity. Some refer to this creativity as "co-creation" with God. Things often just come to you while meditating. By using meditation, we can step away from our "hammer-mill" existence. It's like having a sanctuary. And you get all that from not doing anything? Wow!

This is the easiest way to pray there is. You don't have to do anything. Not even think. In fact, that's the point.

We are so addicted to the business of life that we feel we can't afford to waste any time. We believe that we must account for every second, of every day, of our lives. But for meditation we must "waste time." But you'll find it no waste of time. You'll do more for yourself in ten minutes meditating than anything else you try all day.

Try it. It's simple. Here's how it works:

- Sit in the upright position with feet on the floor and hands in your lap, alone, somewhere where you won't be disturbed for five or ten minutes.

Close your eyes. Sit in a closet if you have to. Hide! Or in your car in a quiet parking lot.
- You will be bombarded with thoughts. But as they pop up in your mind (and this is the key) acknowledge them, but then send them away. Imagine that you're putting them on a cloud as it drifts by, or on a train, or on a leaf floating down a stream.
- There will be noises: birds, dogs, traffic, airplanes… acknowledge them and let them go too, just like the thoughts.
- Your body will talk to you: itching, gurgling, breathing, maybe pain. Acknowledge these feelings and try to let them go the same way—put them on a departing train, a leaf in a stream. If you have to shift yourself for comfort, or scratch, go ahead, then resume.
- Many find concentrating on the in-and-out of their breathing helpful.
- You can imagine that you are somewhere you remember for its beauty and serenity.
- You will notice that the thoughts begin to peter out. That is the simple goal of meditation.
- With your eyes closed, and as you get into it, you may see purple colors and movement. This is normal for your retinas to be still trying to send images to your brain. You can actually concentrate on those movements and colors to enhance your contemplative state.

It's not a relaxation exercise, although it may be relaxing.

It leads to a "neutral state." That's the point you're looking for. Where distractions are temporarily suspended, and your big brain quits its incessant chatter.

Some call this neutral state "Nirvana." The concept of Nirvana can be understood using a glass of water as an example: If you add lemon and sugar to a glass of water it is good. If you add dung to the glass of water it is bad. The water is "Nirvana." It's just water, neither good nor bad. Life is life, neither good nor bad. Meditation gets you to "just water."

God is there in the "Nirvana." We are adding sugar and lemon, or dung. Quit adding anything, and there will be God. And you will communicate with each other.

With meditation, you want to divert the mind from instinctual desires like hunger, anger, fear, or fatigue. You want to divert your mind also from material inclinations like: my car needs gas; what's for dinner? I should be studying/cutting the grass/doing laundry, etc. Some people have so many voices going off in their head it's even hard for them to decide where to sit in a restaurant. (No wonder so many use drugs and alcohol to dull the self-talk.)

It's not self-hypnosis, but you may feel an altered state of euphoric consciousness.

The more you practice meditating, the quicker you "get there" and the more satisfying it becomes. Just like learning to play the piano, your brain gets better and better at meditation with practice.

You can look at a picture of a bicycle. Read about bicycles. Watch a movie about bicycles. But until you get on a bicycle, you won't get it. Some never try a bike. Some never try meditation.

There are other ways to aid in meditation:

Using a ***Mantra***:

Silence is odd—it disturbs us. Repetitive sounds may help when our minds are so confused that we cannot think.

Sitting is best. (Lying down tends to put you to sleep—which is OK too.) Get comfortable. It doesn't matter where you are, just as long as you can close your eyes. (You may want to close them only 2/3 of the way.) You don't have to sit like a Buddha. I can even do this during an airplane journey.

A "mantra" is simply a sound which includes verbal repetition, kind of like chanting. You use the sounds and repetitions to make the mind contemplative. Kind of a vibration.

Dr. Wayne Dyer (author of *Your Erroneous Zones* and many other self-help books)[4] taught me this way of meditation at a lecture once. He learned it from a guru in the Far East. He had the whole audience meditating in minutes. I have used it ever since. He used two soothing and comforting sounds that are found universally in all languages. One is the "mmm" sound; and the other is the "ahh" sound:

"Mmm:" Mom. Home. Yum.

---

4   *Your Erroneous Zones*, 1976, Avon Books, Dr. Wayne W. Dyer.

"Ahhh:" Father. Abba. God. Dad. Allah.

Close your eyes. Take a deep breath and exhale saying "ahhh" until you are ready to take another breath. Repeat over and over with each exhale. Experiment to find a note that kind of resonates in your head. Change pitch and volume as you go until you find that tone that feels right. Or, as you exhale, make a humming noise, "mmm", instead of the "ahhh" noise. Repeat over and over. Or you can alternate the ahhh and mmm.

You will be pleasantly surprised how each cycle brings you back from pop-up thoughts. That is the key to mantra meditation; allowing random thoughts to enter your stream of conscience, but moving them on with each breath cycle. You can still imagine placing the thoughts on clouds, leaves floating down a stream, or a slow-passing train with the doors open into empty boxcars. Or imagine sitting in a room alone and someone walks in, takes the thought from you, then leaves through another door carrying it away.

Let thoughts surface, acknowledge them, and then let them go; send them on their way.

Wait patiently to see what happens. Pretty soon you'll run out of thoughts and "be there," in the meditative state. I know I'm there when, with my eyes closed, I start seeing moving cloudlike purple shapes, and am kind of absentmindedly letting things surface then go on by, not a clue what those thoughts were a second later. Who knows what your "there" will be like, but at some point you may stop the humming altogether, and be "blissed-out."

It doesn't have to go on long to achieve the refreshed, clearedhead relief. Take five minutes for yourself and just try it. If I have a really good meditative session, I may come out of it after only ten minutes, but it seems way longer. You get better at it, as you go. If you do it right, you wake up like a chicken in the morning; with a blank slate!

Speaking of morning, that time of day is a good time to meditate (before your mind overflows with the day's trash can full of angst). Where you do it doesn't matter. Stop in a church, funeral home, or cemetery parking lot on the way to work, and meditate for ten or twenty minutes in the morning in your car. There is something profoundly moving and timeless about those sorts of places. It sounds a little strange, but at least you won't be disturbed there. What a great way to start the day; time just for yourself, before you give yourself away for the rest of the day.

What do you do with your hands? Make an "O" with thumb and forefinger and interlock the two "Os" of each hand. It is similar to the infinity symbol. Or put your hands flat on top of each other, palms up or down, just below the navel, with thumbs touching and elbows straight out opposite each other. Or just rest your hands in your lap anyway they fall, holding each other or not.

There are all kinds of other activities you can use as a mantra to help get you into a meditative state: ringing a gong, beating a drum, dancing, cutting the grass, cleaning, jogging, walking, watching incense smoke rise, doodling, watching a wood fire, doing cardio on a stationary bike, swimming laps, etc.

Religious phrases can be used as mantras too: "Hail Mary full of grace; Lord have mercy; The Lord is my shepherd; Thy will be done; Via con Dios (Go with God.); Our Father who art in Heaven, etc."

A variation of the God-is-great part of the three-part prayer can become a mantra. *You* are exalted, wonderful, magnificent, absolute, boundless, marvelous, super, amazing, worthy… Thank you, thank you, thank you….

And don't forget music. There are thousands of pieces available that aid in contemplative thought, rest, meditation, and prayer. Music helps drown out the monkey talk. Covers up distractions. Focuses your attention away from brain-noise. Try a Gregorian chant… Enya… a symphony… electronic music… hymns… modern praise music. Also, there are recordings of whales, rain, trains, rippling streams, and so on, to quiet the self-talk.

***PRAYER TIP #8: While jogging, walking, or working out, try saying phrases or words (like a mantra) in-between each breath, or step, or group of steps. (Runner's high?) Or each repetition of lifting weights, rowing, and so on: praise God; love You; thank You; love me; serenity; let-go/let-God….***

***Buddhism*** offers the mantra that is popular for meditation: ***"Om Mani Padme Hum."***

It is easy to say and powerful because it supposedly contains the essence of the entire teachings of the Tibetan Buddhists.

According to the Dalai Lama the six syllables "purify" things that are not good things to have if you want to be like Buddha:

1. *"Om" purifies possessiveness. Helps you become more generous.*
2. *"Ma" expels jealousy and lust. Helps you not be so prideful; more ethical.*
3. *"Ni" purifies passion and desire. Helps you practice tolerance and patience.*
4. *"Pad" reduces stupidity and prejudice. Helps you get closer to perfection.*
5. *"Me" purifies concentration. Helps with focus.*
6. *"Hum" takes away aggression and hatred. Helps give you wisdom.*

Whatever… you don't have to know the meaning for it to work. (It's all a mystery to me.)

The Dalai Lama provides a short in-depth analysis on a web page: <u>The meaning of Om Mani Padme Hum</u>.[5] He concludes his discussion with, "Thus the six syllables provide an indivisible union of method and wisdom, so you can transform your impure body,

---

5  www.cirle-of-light.com/mantras/om

speech, and mind, into the pure body, speech, and mind, of a Buddha."

Add a pinch of incense, a cup of music, a spoonful of candlelight; it makes a great meditation.

Repeat the mantra over and over with each exhaled breath: *"ohm…mah…nee…pahd…may…hum."*

(Nice isn't it, how the phrase is full of *mmm's* and *ahhh's*?)

Use **Visualization** to meditate.

How about going to a "happy place?"

Quiet yourself by imagining being in a setting you remember that helped you to be relaxed, calm, and free of distractions.

One spring, on a walk in the mountains, I found a small, clear, bubbling stream that circled halfway around a small grassy meadow, maybe thirty feet in diameter. The grass was new and fluorescent green. It looked like it had been mowed because the length of the brand-new blades was the same. Scattered in the tiny meadow were yellow-green ferns. Multicolored granite rocks were partially covered here and there with red and orange lichen, along with fuzzy soft dark green moss. Toddler wildflowers excitedly bounced and waved with gentle breezes. Like an impressionist's pastel painting there were pink aster, white bachelor's buttons, reddish purple daisies, blue lupine, yellow-orange paintbrush, pastel bluebells, and purple lavender.

A small number of bees busily harvested pollen. Two pale blue butterflies swooped and fluttered about each other. The whole setting was surrounded by explosive pinkish-purple just having bloomed red bud trees, and astonishingly white Dogwoods in flower, elderly tall pine trees, and closely packed slim Aspen trees. All the trees had brand-new leaves twinkling in the clean breeze and bright sun. I could imagine the trees holding on to each other by their roots in the compost from their foliage from all the years and seasons past, as they sipped spring's melted snow runoff.

All this color and nature was backdropped by a cerulean blue sky dotted with occasional puffy white clouds. I could smell and hear the breeze wafting through the pines. The bubbling stream was mesmerizing; its rocks and moss spectacular.

To this day I can still visualize that little alpine meadow in my mind. I can smell the pines, flowers, and forest-floor compost. Hear the air and water. Feel the warm sun on my face and through the fabric covering my shoulders and back. I cleared my mind and meditated there that day. I can still feel the soft moss on my palms as I sat there cross-legged, eyes closed, my breath moving gently in and out. It was ***awesome***!

I go back there in my mind sometimes to meditate. That's what I mean by visualization. Closing your eyes and revisiting a place in your mind as a way to get into meditation.

You can get inspiration for visualization in other ways besides remembering a place that was of special beauty. There's even beauty in a store's housewares department—glass, vases, pottery, fabrics, etc. Flower shops. Gourmet food sections at the grocery store. Five minutes in the fruit and vegetable section of the supermarket can be a meditation of sorts, or at least a prayer of awe and thanksgiving.

Sometimes during meditation, I visualize leaving Earth, imagining what the Hubble telescope might be seeing right now in space. We've all seen those images of swirling galaxies, star clusters, not to mention the moon. Talk about *awesome*! Talk about unknowable.

Be like a dump truck driver. Just sit there and get filled up.

You can go to an awesome beach. Or canoe an awesome lake. Take an awesome motorcycle ride. Use yoga. Martial arts. Jog. Shoot baskets. In your mind or for real. A friend swore she was never closer to the spirit world than when she cleaned house to thumping pop-rock.

Meditation is something you may already be doing.

***PRAYER TIP #9****: **We all say "awesome" a lot. Sunsets can be awesome. Waterfalls can be awesome. Completed football passes can be awesome. A kiss can be awesome. Think about it. These awesome things are gifts. Not ordinary things. Spectacular things. I call awesome things like this "God Stuff." We mere mortals just can't put together an awesome sunset. Maybe you're praying every time you say the word "awesome?"*

# CHAPTER SEVEN

**PRAYER AND SCIENCE**

Many have science at the heart of their belief system, to the exclusion of God, not seeing the compatibility of the two. With science curriculum education paths dominating their lives, some just plain haven't had time for much else except study and work in their chosen field. Countless of these people (author included) at some point however find unknowns at the ends of their discipline's pathway—mystery, ambiguity, obscurity, inscrutability, enigma, impenetrability....

Many scientists admit that they can be enlightened only just so far, and conclude that there is something inexplicable going on that they're never going to figure out. That there is something beyond human understanding, whether it's in the field of chemistry, physics, biology, reproduction, electricity, space, etc.

Answers just lead to further questions until there is an unanswerable one. (Your answers questioned?)

Einstein, in his own words, revealed that he had "a humble admiration for an unlimited Superior Spirit, which reveals itself in the few slight details that we are able to perceive with our frail and feeble minds."

The study of quantum mechanics and "The Big Bang," dead-ends in mystery for all who go there. As new theories are proposed, new experiments unveiled, new depths probed, physicists just find physics not behaving like physics should. Stephen Hawking in his book *Black Holes and Baby Universes* reflected that even if he did succeed in discovering how the universe began, where it's going, what it's doing, and how it's doing it, he still doesn't know why it began.

I have found that the mysteries at the end of roads in physics, medicine, astronomy, etc., are just fuel for my spirituality. The mysticism actually makes it easier for me to pray. Kind of a *wow, what an awesome God!*

So, here is some awesome God science stuff to maybe make you prayerful:

- On earth carbon molecules get recycled continually being reused in new life forms of all kinds. Science reminds us that our physical forms are made from (and will return to) the continually recycling supply of ingredients in the universe. Subatomic particles somehow (mysteriously) have coalesced into life-using carbon. Science reminds us that what we are made of, will live on

in some state, or form, maybe energy… or maybe matter, in infinite time. The elements in us will be recycled. Maybe another big-bang will start us all over again. And again. And again… who knows? Who set off the big-bang in the first place? Why?
- If you could somehow "mark" every electron circling the nucleus of all of the atoms in a single glass of water, then dump that glass of water in any ocean, tomorrow, at least one of those "marked" electrons would be found in every glass of water you dipped out of any ocean, anywhere in the world. Electrons really get around.
- If the nucleus of a hydrogen atom were the size of a basketball, the electrons circling around it would be twenty miles away! What's in all that space in atoms? Fifteen billion years ago the subatomic parts that make up your body were scattered all across the universe in a cloud. We have one hundred trillion cells cooperating in our body made from stuff from the universe. How did all this come together to allow you to create a poem, watch a movie, or pray?
- We have billions of bacteria living in our intestines. (And it's dark in there.) Something like ten to the fourteenth power. That's a whole universe inside each mammal on the planet. Can you believe all the mouths He feeds? (There's millions and millions of bacteria living on our feet too!) Speaking of sheer numbers how about this? The collective weight of all the ants in the

world is more than the collective weight of all the people in the world!
- How come DNA vibrates around 80 billion cycles a second? How come light acts like a particle sometimes, but like a wave at other times? Did you know that matter and energy change roles? That's like software turning into hardware, and back again. Nothing to something to nothing. That's creation? One group of scientists said an electron behaves like a particle on Mondays, Wednesdays, and Fridays; and on Tuesdays, Thursdays, and Saturdays it behaves like a wave. On Sunday the theorists simply prayed.
- If reproduction is the ultimate goal of Mother Nature, then apple trees and potato vines, are the hands down winners. (Then there's rats!)
- Then there's gravity. And fire. Meditate on a candle flame for a while. (No one has explained gravity fully.)
- How about radio, TV, cell phones, radar, X-rays, MRIs, GPS… talk about energy being changed into something… information, sound, images….

Science is sliding away from the concept of our big brain as a machine or computer. Researchers are studying things like emotions, meaning, belief, and consciousness, and are demonstrating that love is necessary for brain development. Genes and cells are not simply selfish little survivors. Moral intuitions and instincts for fairness and empathy are real and seem to transcend boundaries of self, rising toward a larger presence. Self is not what we are. Instead, self is a process involving relationships and attachments, and of course "cosmic-two-by-fours" knocking some "sense" into your brain.

Science and mysticism are holding hands. Those that see the invisible can see the impossible. Prayer and meditation show you the invisible, so you can see the impossible.

What is real anyway? Some golf and basketball coaches know the brain can't tell the difference between a really good visualization, and actual practice. The classic experiment goes like this:

One group of basketball players practiced for a week, and another group did nothing but visualize taking shots at a basket. Both groups were measured and, depending on the reference, the group that did nothing but visualize, did better, or at least as good, as the ones that actually practiced.

**Thoughts in mind create like kind.** Our brains are more than processors of a binary algorithm. Are we co-creators somehow? Prayer and meditation are another way to create. To process. To see the un-seeable. Like an X-ray. Like a TV show. Like a cell phone call. It turns out everything is just energy. Prayer is too? Are we actually making energy and sending it out there when we pray?

There is a God we know, and a God we don't know. Prayer and meditation bring you closer to both.

# CHAPTER EIGHT

**THE LORD'S PRAYER**

Why re-invent the wheel? There are lots of prayers already written. Without a doubt the most widely used of all is The Lord's Prayer.

On any given Easter Sunday it is estimated that 2 billion Christians read, recite, or sing the short prayer in hundreds of languages. It is a golden thread through the colorful fabric of diverse theological differences, and the endless varieties of worship, that makes up Christianity. It has remained virtually unchanged for two millennia. It is said by non-Christians alike. (God loves diversity.) The Lord's Prayer language has been tested and refined, and says what we are thinking and feeling, better than we can express it ourselves.

(I've used the Lord's Prayer, or parts of it, as a mantra. Said over and over, it calms, centers, and comforts me. Like the "Om Mani Padme Hum" prayer for Buddhists.)

Most of us say it mechanically, by rote, not thinking about its meaning. The Lord's Prayer can say different things to different people, at different times, during different needs. This is my spin on it: *(And please forgive me, God, for not being able to credit the countless teachers whose ideas I have taken here for my own.)*

- *OUR FATHER*; The relationship between God and man is that of father and child. (So, sit on his lap and babble.) Interestingly, the case could be made that the offspring is of the same nature as the Creator (Father and son). So, there is some Divine in us too. And guess what? We're all brothers and sisters too!
- *WHICH ART IN HEAVEN*; God is in Heaven… and man is on Earth… and we have our own roles in the grand scheme.
- *HALLOWED BE THY NAME*; Hallowed means holy. Holy means spiritually perfect; untainted by evil or sin; regarded with great respect or reverence. Thy nature is altogether good.
- *THY KINGDOM COME*; Some think this is a command to spread the word. (Evangelism.) Another interpretation is that it is our work to bring God's ideas into being in our earthly realm. Whatever floats your boat. (Or ark?)
- *THY WILL BE DONE;* This is an addendum to the previous clause; a statement that Earth

is to be under divine command. This is also a declaration like, "let go… let God." Repeating, "Thy will be done," over and over, makes a great mantra for meditation, or can just be comforting during times of stress, fear, loss, frustration, or any adversity.
- *AS IT IS IN HEAVEN*; This could mean make Earth like Heaven; or it could mean His will will be done in both Heaven and Earth.
- *GIVE US THIS DAY OUR DAILY BREAD*; Children look to their parents as we should look to God… to supply our bread (every day). And "bread" here could mean not only food for the body, but food for the soul.
- *AND FORGIVE US OUR TRESPASSES, AS WE FORGIVE THOSE THAT TRESPASS AGAINST US*; Asking for, and giving, forgiveness is a staple in all religions, and is a ubiquitous thread that goes through civilization. Treat your neighbors as you would want to be treated. We can't demand our own forgiveness without releasing our brothers and sisters as well.
- *AND LEAD US NOT INTO TEMPTATION*; A plea to help us not to lie, cheat, steal, etc. (The Ten Commandments.) Additionally, as we work down our spiritual path, led by God, we may be tempted to credit ourselves for being a really good "holy-roller-bible-thumper" demigod. This is to remind us not to be self-righteous, or prideful of our spirituality.

- *BUT DELIVER US FROM EVIL*; Well, we all have our own demons.
- *FOR THINE IS THE KINGDOM, AND THE POWER, AND THE GLORY, FOREVER AND EVER.* The "Kingdoms" of Heaven and Earth, and the universe, are created and powered by God. An omnipresence. God is everywhere. Glory? With Him, we will have great happiness, satisfaction, and triumph (glory). Then, finally, we are reminded that all this is timeless… *FOREVER!*
- *AMEN.* "Amen" means you adopt for your own what was said by another. It is a form of affirmation, or confirmation, of the speaker's thoughts. When you say it, you affirm, "I agree." Or, "I take in." Or, "So be it." Some people and ministers say it twice; "I agree… So be it." Amen is employed in the ritual of both Jews and Mohammedans, and was used way before Christianity. A classic example in the Bible is found in Deuteronomy (27:14): "Cursed be he that honoureth not his father and mother, and all the people say Amen." (So… be careful what you say about your mother-in-law.) NOTE: You don't have to use the word Amen at the end of your prayers. Like I said, there are no rules.)

# CHAPTER NINE

**GET YOUR BODY INTO IT**

Just as incense, meditative music, mantras, and candlelight, make it easier to pray, so can the position of the body and hands.

We are a hybrid of spirit and body. We stand up for what we believe. We stand to greet a loved one or friend. We stand in the presence of guests, or to show chivalry, or respect. Little children hang their heads when caught in a lie, or are embarrassed. We wave. We dance, leap, and spin. We communicate with our hands and bodies— not just our minds and voices.

Choosing a posture, or position of the head, or hands, helps prayerfulness. Matching your body to your thoughts makes it easier to pray, which is what this book is all about.

To see how it works, try this: think up a prayer using

the Please help/God is great/Thanks—basic prayer. Anything, like help me with work, a relationship, or for a friend in need. Then say the same prayer using five different postures:

1. **Stand with hands uplifted** and open, head up, eyes open. This is a joyful posture. We stand and shout at sports events and concerts. It feels good to stand and send out thanks and adoration.
2. **Stand with arms hanging** and hands clasped in front of you, head bowed, eyes down. This was the posture of a shackled prisoner brought before the king. It is a position of submission, surrender, and asking.
3. **Kneeling**, hands clasped, with head up or down. This was the posture for requesting favors from a king. It is another position of submission, compliance, and asking.
4. **On your knees with your forehead on the floor**, or lying on your stomach, forehead on the ground; palms up, or flat in front of you. This was the posture for begging favors from a king when one is literally without standing, and is desperate. It is a sign of humility. It is still used in eastern churches and temples where they don't have pews, but plenty of rugs.
5. **Sitting**, head down, hands clasped. This is the position for receiving instruction, or contemplation/meditation.

All the positions work for asking for help, giving thanks, and praise. But aren't they different in feeling? Try a *Please-help* prayer flat on your chest at 3:00 a.m. when you're suffocating during a "dark night of the soul." Try a *Thank-You* prayer standing, with your arms flung high and wide after a kiss, passing an exam, making a sale, or knowing a loved one made it through surgery. Then try kneeling. You'll see how it works.

# CHAPTER TEN

### WHEN AND WHERE TO PRAY

Sometimes the *When* and *Where* picks you.

I was trailering my horse, Johnny, home after an *awesome* ride on trails in the woods around a lake with friends. It was a beautiful early spring Sunday afternoon. I took a wrong turn trying to get back to the interstate. You can't just do U-turns easily with a horse trailer. I finally got turned around and backtracked. I heard Johnny whinny a few times wondering what I was doing. We were both tired and hungry. I came around a bend that I had already gone around twenty minutes prior, and two cars were stopped in the middle of the road, with their hazard lights on, and doors wide open.

People were gathered by the side of the road, and I saw a motorcycle upside down in the trees next to the road. I sat in my car as an ambulance came screaming to a halt. The road was blocked, people were aiding the victim and I was kind of miffed at having another delay. Johnny was stomping.

There was another motorcycle parked and a rider in leathers was nervously pacing. Suddenly I felt something was really wrong. I knew that these two motorcyclers, just moments ago, were enjoying a beautiful spring ride on their bikes in the country. I felt a wave of compassion for them cover me. The one on the ground had not moved. Something told me to pray... and really earnestly.

I directed my palms toward the scene and asked God to "please come." That someone really needed Him. "Please come be with this injured person. Help him." I said it over and over. That was all I could think to say. I wished I had a really good "injured person" prayer. I was kind of ashamed that I couldn't do better. My face was flushed. I could feel its heat. My hands were trembling. I felt short of breath— my chest tight. I closed my eyes tight. I kept saying, "This person really needs you, God."

Finally, they got him on the stretcher and into the ambulance, and I was on my way. I knew he was being taken care of. I kind of felt a little embarrassed getting all worked up like I did. I hoped no one saw me acting like that. (I'm still not totally comfortable praying in public.) I forgot about it.

I touched the TV remote the next morning seconds after waking up. The very first thing I heard the newsman say was, "A motorcycle accident on the lake road yesterday afternoon, resulted in the death of the rider, a Mr.—"

I was there! *I was supposed to be there.* I didn't know I was essentially doing Last Rites! I was praying for a guy who was dying. I can only say thank God I decided to pray. It was a BIG PRAYER, and I didn't even know it. Someone was there to say a prayer over a man during the last few moments of his life. It was me. A complete stranger.

I knew it didn't matter that I didn't use complete sentences. That the prayer didn't have a beginning or end. That it was in shorthand; that I didn't even know what I was saying.

Where is a good place to pray? Sometimes you don't pick the place—the place picks you.

*Church* is a good place to pray. *(Duh!)*

Go to a designated place of prayer. Hire a professional. If you haven't been for a while, maybe you haven't found the right church.

No matter what religious service you attend, in whatever church you go to, there is a collective, exponential, and lavish, spiritual event going on there. Just be carried along with the stream effortlessly. Sit back and let someone else maneuver the excursion boat, or drive the tour bus.

These religious leaders are trained to pray. And their prayers are really, really good. Surgeons are trained to do all kinds of repair work on your body. You're only expected to put a Band-Aid on. God doesn't expect you to pray like a professional.

Church, temple, synagogue, mosque... all have one really good advantage: you don't have to think up the prayers there. You don't have to reinvent the wheel. They "spoon-feed" you spirituality. It's easy praying—kind of another "let go, let God" thing. We're "lost sheep," and sometimes we just need a shepherd, and a sheep dog.

Some of us "try on" spirituality at church and just plain don't like it. Maybe we think it's because every church is full of hypocrites. Or you have gotten tired of sitting there not knowing where you're at in the program. And the hymns... they're literally from last century (maybe even a lot of centuries ago). Or you were dragged there by someone which makes you a "common-law" churchgoer, only there "due to partner." You can't help feeling like everyone is looking down on you from a loftier position. And then there's the holier-than-thou, sanctimonious, patronizing, "member" that circles you like you were prey. They are *way too nice*. And the incense makes your head stuffy. And you have to dress up. And they shame you for money.

Maybe the preacher preaches that you specifically are a sinner and need to be saved. And you don't have a clue what being saved means. And you're pretty sure you don't even want to be saved. And you don't know for sure if you were baptized as an infant so you're afraid to even be there since the last thing you want is to be the center of attention when that issue surfaces. (The lightning strike.)

Maybe you want to believe and to feel God's presence, maybe pray, even go to church, but can't deal with those miracles and revelations that you think border on the bizarre, and you hate arguing about moral issues with condemning authority figures, who impose their version on you as the "one and only." (It has been estimated that of all churchgoers, only 20 percent "believe" in their church's teachings and doctrines, and 80 percent are "not sure." You're in good company if you're in the not-sure group.)

So, you end up one of the millions of "unchurched." "The church has many that God does not. God has many the church has not." St. Augustine (AD 345-430)

All the different churches and faiths, despite their philosophical differences, have a similar objective: emphasizing human improvement, love, respect for others, and sharing other people's suffering.

Organized religion? Going to church? Even if you don't completely buy into their beliefs, it definitely has its benefits. It's the easiest place to pray there is, because you don't have to do the driving. Let a professional chauffer you around.

If traditional services chill you, try a "contemporary" service. They are often at convenient times, Saturday and Sunday evenings. They are usually informal. You can wear jeans. They often have a band playing upbeat modern songs. You can hide in the back. You can duck out after a while. You don't have to be a member, or be confirmed, or be baptized, or have a clue what's going on. These contemporary services are often easy to follow because many use video and multimedia equipment to lead you along. You can hop around from church to church... sometimes the biggest churches are the best because of anonymity.

God doesn't care how you come to him. Dipping in and out of organized religion is a great way to try on new ideas during your "spiritual walk."

It's amazing, but almost every time you go to church you hear something you need to hear or that will help you get through the following week. It often answers prayers you didn't even know you needed to pray.

This is not a book about religion. It's not a book about churches. Or evangelism. Or conversion. Or doctrine. Or thumping Bibles. Or denomination. Or deity. It's about how easy it is to pray. It's *really* easy to pray if you can just walk into some place of prayer and accept what is offered at least to a degree. Church offers delightful, meaningful "spoon-fed" prayer available just for the taking.

Make prayer really easy; let someone else do it.

Thinking about trying a *new religion*? Longing for a whole new start? Converting to something different?

I heard the Dalai Lama speak in India. He's all about Buddhism, of course.

But when someone asked him what religion he recommended, he said it's best to stay with the one you were born into. He explained that they all accomplish the same thing and that they all have faults and inconsistencies. They are manmade and therefore subject to man's foibles. He said that if we put too much emphasis on our own philosophy, religion, or theory, and are too attached to it, and try to impose it on other people, "it makes trouble."

He stressed if you started as a Christian, stay Christian. "There are riches at your own banquet." Maybe just "season" it a little. As opposed to completely switching to Buddhism, Judaism, Islam, Hinduism, Cherokee, Zulu, Muslim, Jainism, Sikhism, Daoism, Confucianism, capitalism, or cannibalism.

There are three basic categories of religion: 1. PRIMAL—like Native American, African; 2. ASIAN—like Buddhism, Hindu, Confucianism; 3. MONOTHEASTIC—like Islam, Judaism, Christianity, and Save-The-Whales. There's something for everyone. They're definitely fun to study. Hop around, mix and match. Make up your own versions. Lots of people have done just that, including me.

Our world is a rich tapestry of diverse peoples and cultures, and with different cultures come diverse roads to God. God loves diversity; look at nature. So, there are a lot of religions.

The Dalai Lama counseled again and again that human sensibilities and cultures are too varied to justify a single way to the truth. He said Buddhism and Christianity are so different that those who call themselves "Buddhist-Christians" are trying "to put a yak's head on a sheep's body." But he added that no one can say Christians have nothing to learn from Asia, and vice-versa.

He said, "Christianity! It's like a big house with many rooms." Then he added, "It's the same in all religions." It's best to stay more or less with the culture that you are accustomed to. Certain religious holidays are observed, for example. There is a comfort zone, he said, that comes with familiarity. Study world religions. Look for the common threads that course through all religions: man's humanity to man; forgiveness; believing in a higher power; charity; and the good works that percolate through all religions. But, and this was his reasoning, it is **way easier to pray** using the structure you were raised in, and you live in now—similar to the comfort you have with the language you grew up with. Your brain is literally programmed to work certain ways in the background and conditions that you grew up in. You may find it very difficult to do something new.

Become a Buddhist monk if you want. No one cares, and neither does God. (Well, your mother might care.)

But, if you want prayer to be easier, stick with the one you came with. I don't know what the intentions of Christ and Mohammed were, but I know they both, at least, just wanted us to know God and to pray. Make it simple on yourself. Use what you have already. You don't have to learn a new language, or reinvent the wheel.

And remember, there are no rules for prayer no matter what culture or faith you were born into. You can pray anywhere, anytime, and anything you say or think can be a prayer. And now, after reading this little book, you have the: Please help; Thanks; God is great— prayer.

Get into prayer easier by creating a physical **Special Place**. Create a little **Sanctuary** for yourself—a corner of a spare bedroom, or a spot just for you in the basement, or attic. All you're looking for is a place to get you into the spirit of prayer and meditation easily. An instant get-in-the-proper-mood place. You can pray at a sports event, but in your little place it will probably go better for you, and be *easier*.

You need light, but extravagant use of light destroys the feel. In dimness, the hard lines of old furniture, injured or unfinished walls and ceilings, and glass and metal, soften and are muted. In Galileo's time there was no light from towns and cities in the sky. The Milky Way was so bright it cast shadows. Light was from candles and oil lamps.

(Isn't there something positively elegant about a lonely light bulb softly illuminating the porch of a distant farmhouse as glimpsed from a car, or train window, at night?)

Darkness has its own beauty, and lends itself to meditation because of the decrease in external stimuli.

Candlelight flickering in the dark is jerky and its shadows bounce. But a candle behind thin fabric, or a shade, sheds a cloudy translucent radiance casting no jerky shadows, and leaves the recesses of your room in the dark. The screen in front of the candle takes the light and envelops it gently, like thin snow at dusk. Or like gray, cloud-filtered light through a dripping spotted rainy window. I love light shaded by different papers, plastic, or glass. Things like jewels, colored glass, jade, quartz, gold jewelry... seem to dance in candlelight with a glow deep from within them, but in bright light, they just reflect.

You've noticed that as if by enchantment, your lover's beauty, or handsomeness, soars by candlelight. Also, wine and food absorb the light instead of reflecting it. (Candlelight dinner!)

A single low-wattage bulb, or Christmas lights, behind a piece of stained glass or a translucent shade, will give off a vague translucence. The dim shadows make beauty instead of starkness, glare, and curvelessness.

Civilization went from candle to oil lamp, from oil lamp to gaslight, then to electric light, making sure we eradicated even the smallest shadow. But darkness is original. It is inevitable. It is mysterious... of the spirit world. You can immerse yourself in it. You can imagine things in the dark and shadows that you can't in bright lights. A potted plant seems to float, and its flaws and tears and browns dissolve. In the dark, you can listen. We talk too much. (Especially Christians!)

Use some gold—the color. Its reflective properties retain a certain brilliance even in the dark, whereas silver and other metals quickly lose their gloss. As you move past a gold silk oriental screen, or a gold painted vase or wooden chair, the dull sleepy luster suddenly gleams reflecting even in the dimmest light. I can see why gold was used on statues of Buddha, and gold leaf used in cathedrals, in the dark past. It was a source of illumination in dark indoor space. It is a mystery to me why it works.

On a small table in my prayer area, I put a collection of things that have special meaning to me. Travel has been of great importance to me.... I love looking for spiritual common threads in different cultures. I have a little dark mahogany carved frog I got in North Vietnam; a tiny bottle of sand I gathered next to the Great Pyramid; coral from Cuba and the Bahamas, an insignificant rock I picked up at the foot of the Great Wall in China; a tiny red piece of plaster I found near the foundation that the Taj Mahal sits on; a prayer shawl from Jerusalem; a Buddhist prayer flag from Northern India; a piece of gravel from Stonehenge; stuff from all over Europe and Scandinavia, Canada, Alaska, Mexico, South America, Africa, the Middle East, the West Indies, etc.

Also, I have a globe handy. Just spinning it gently sparks mystery and spirituality for me.

Additionally, I have a Rosary, Cross, Star of David, a copy of the Serenity Prayer, prayer beads, squeezable stress releasers, and all kinds of oriental and Native Indian stuff. (Note: prayer beads, or a Rosary, can be excellent meditation tools.)

The point is to have things in your "sanctuary" that inspire you, move you, remind you of spirit, and project you into thinking spiritually. They make it easier to get in the mood for prayer and meditation. Using material objects to help you focus for worship is not idol worship. It just helps focus on the mysterious. It's just atmosphere.

The Hebrews place of worship was a large elaborate tent called a tabernacle. When they couldn't go to church, they wore individual' shawls that were a "little tent." Your own private sanctuary—an intimate place of privacy—is your little tabernacle.

I keep a little hot water maker and a variety of teas and snacks in my sanctuary. (Sometimes I need to eat, not pray.) I also have dozens of "Daily Readers." These have a one-page thought or message, with a prayer, for each day of the year. Like: *Daily Reflections*[6]; *Discovering Joy*[7]; *Look To This Day*[8]; *The Chakras*[9]; *Courage To Change*[10]; and so on. They offer a quick spiritual thought to help me focus.

I sit cross-legged on several cushions on the floor, at a table, or rocked back in a cushioned chair. (I believe in "comfort" in my sanctuary… not hair-shirts, self-flagellation, and a crown of thorns.)

I have handy "space music," chants, ocean sounds, rain sounds, and so on. And some incense, of course.

I have pictures of my loved ones. Some Tibetan

---

6   Daily Reflections, Alcoholic Anonymous World Services, New York, N.Y.
7   Discovering Joy, Bethany House Publishers, Minneapolis, Minnesota, 555438.
8   Look To This Day, Alan L Roeck, Harper & Row, Publishers, San Francisco.
9   The Chakras, C.W. Leadbeater, Quest Books, Wheaton, Illinois, Chennai (Madras), India.
10  Courage to Change, A-Anon Family Group Headquarters, Inc.

bells, and gongs, brass bowls that ring, chimes, drums, a flute, etc. It's always being added to. Sometimes I receive little gifts from others. I give stuff away. And trade. (It's fun to shop for these special things when you travel.)

And I have a Bible. There are lots of different kinds. I use the *Quest Study Bible*[11]. It gives editorial comment, explanations, history and background, applications to modern times, and so on, all through it. I like the Psalms. They are short and each has a message still pertinent to today.

Like:

*Have mercy on me oh God,*
*I have taken refuge, as you*
*Show us your mercy, and give us your salvation.*
*The Lord is my shepherd, and I shall not want.*

At the time of the writing of the Psalms, historians of the Middle East adjusted their stories to get the message delivered. Remember the art of storytelling is to make a story magnificent and memorable. Sometimes they exaggerated. They are poetry, rather than doctrine, or factual essays. They are full of parable, fiction with an outer story, inner meaning.

To me the Bible is not to be taken literally all the time. The same passages may even mean one thing to me today and something else to me tomorrow. It's full

---

[11] The Quest Study Bible, Zondervan Publishing House, Grand Rapids, Michigan, 49530.

of imaginative symbolism, allegory, imagery, figures of speech, exaggerations, and metaphors. (Let the Bible literalists pursue their path. Honoring a person where they are does not dishonor you.)

The point of all this is to urge you to create a special place... with visuals, sounds, smells, objects, and reading material to help you connect with the spirit world. It's just another way to make praying easier. It gives you a place to look forward to, and know you can rest in. It gradually takes on a holiness of its own. By cultivating the right environment, you can instantly open yourself so that God can be with you.

I can pray anywhere, anytime—from planes to mountain meadows, or sitting at stoplights. But my sanctuary is just plain fun. It makes it way easier to pray. And that's what this book is about.

**Praying in the *Middle of the Night*?**
Monasteries sometimes have prayer services in the middle of the night. I've been on retreats where we were awakened at 3:00 a.m. to pray (an Episcopal Cursillo). You'd be surprised how clear your mind is then. And falling back to sleep comes easily. It's sort of like it didn't happen. If anything, I felt more refreshed in the morning. I wake up around three in the morning regularly, and feel God's presence. Many I have interviewed putting together this little book report the same.

I lost a business to a flood. I didn't know how I would be able to take care of my family. I felt defeated. Despair crackled through my soul. I was devastated. Night after night I woke around 3:00 a.m., worry and fear consuming me, maybe or maybe not falling back into restless sleep. A lot of stuff that worked for me before didn't work anymore: drinking, the same friends....

One night around 3:00 a.m., I gave up. I got down on my knees by the bed, elbows on the bed, forehead in my hands, and told God I was giving everything to Him. I just said out loud, "I'm done. You take it from here." Over and over.

I woke up a little later, still on my knees, upper body draped across the mattress, head lying on my hands. Very softly, but not a whisper, I heard only one word: my name. Just that word. Crystal clear. I was bathed in the strongest, whitest, light I have ever seen, but it did not hurt my eyes at all. At that moment I felt what I guess they call "rapture;" euphoric happiness and delight. God spoke my name! I can still hear him calling my name that night to this day. My eyes are tearing as I write this.

My agonizing heart and trudging brain rested from the turbulence. Even though it was a fleeting time of calm, it was so deeply appreciated.

Nothing improved. In fact, things got worse. I even got kind of a morbid fascination with pondering what horrible thing was going to happen next.

But I had God now. And my "dark night of the soul" never got that dark again. I had a starting place. I didn't feel stranded. (You know you're in a "dark night of the soul" if you know the truth, but are still having the experience.)

Many times, when you get hurt, you don't have a "witness." So, when you get it out to God, it is finally witnessed. It releases you from the enemy of fear and isolation by having someone hear your story. When we share our woundedness, there is something powerful about that. The quiet peace of the middle of the night is a good time. It's easy to be completely honest then.

The next time you wake up in the middle of the night, whether it's 3:00 a.m. or not, instead of worrying, and arranging scenes for the next day, try thinking, or say, a please-help prayer. You don't have to put it in words even. In fact, an unfinished open-ended prayer may be best. Maybe you're not able to sleep anyway, so why not get up, sit by a window in the diffuse light of a streetlamp or the moon, and pray. It is always sleep-inducing.

He's there listening for you.

No one is exempt from problems. I am stunned at the dogged bravery so many people demonstrate just to get through the day. (Handicaps, chronic disease/pain, addictions, unemployment, sick kids, car wrecks, poverty, homelessness…)

There is kind of a negative comfort knowing there are other sufferers besides you. Also, we tend to stay in our rut. We stay in our little corner of hell because it's familiar. We're afraid of change even for the good. Change is like a new pair of slippers. The old ones are falling apart, but we don't want to break in a new pair.

But God will change you one way or the other. He is waiting for you to call. He needs to get in. You may have him barricaded. Sometimes to get something that you want, you have to do something you haven't done. Like pray. Meditate.

The positive comfort is that we all have a God-given power to solve a lot of the problems... if we'll listen.

**PRAYER TIP #10: *The next time you wake up in the middle of the night, tune in the radio station KGOD. At night it comes in with less static. It's a powerful station—heard around the world. It's a call-in show.***

Maybe you've been praying on and off all day but with no answer. Try just **sleeping on it**.

You're really just putting a please-help prayer out there when you go to sleep with something on your mind. You'll often have your answer in the morning. Or at least a direction. Can you name all the problems from yesterday right now? See, you already know how to pray. And it worked. Many of those problems are gone already. Or at least their power over you diminished. You have a different perspective in the morning.

It's amazing what a difference a day makes.

(It's interesting, isn't it, that sometimes it's the clichés that give us solace? You might even call them prayers of a sort: *Trust in God; God works in mysterious ways; There but for the grace of God go I.*)

Prayer just can't get any simpler than this. It's way easier to pray than you think, isn't it? Just go to sleep. Or take a nap.

***PRAYER TIP #11: Just sleep on it. Your subconscious mind knows how to pray even if you don't. Sleep is an alternate state of consciousness. Say a prayer for an answer or direction. Then let God work with you without your stinkin'-thinkin' blocking Him.***

# CHAPTER ELEVEN

**WARNING:
UNINTENDED CONSEQUENCES
MAY HAPPEN WHEN YOU PRAY**

Praying leads to hard, but necessary, work:

- When you choose the spiritual path and you find yourself praying more, beware. Everything not in alignment with your new path will come up demanding attention. This may be discouraging since you think you should be transcending all your baggage full of human desire and suffering.
- What you think is an unresponsive God, you may later find, is a God that provides you in ways we could not have imagined. You may not even see the results of your praying. Or you may not get answers right away. Or you may not get what you

want, but you'll get what you need.
- If you push into something you didn't want to, you may have pushed into God. If you ask for help with your anger, you may get everything that tests your anger. If you ask for help with your patience, you may get everything that tests your patience.
- You can't turn your back to God. No matter which way we turn, we still face God.
- You'll keep re-learning the same lesson until you change. Keep doing what you're doing, and you'll keep getting what you're getting.
- To get something you never had, you have to do something you never did.
- As you become more comfortable in the spiritual world, and less comfortable in the material world, you may lose friends. Your circle may not understand you anymore.
- We're all "spirit" having a human experience. We are all where we are supposed to be on our individual spiritual paths. And it's not the same place for everyone. You may end up with a new circle of friends. The sum total of your thoughts and feelings will change. Your soul will change. Your heart will change. (Your brain is literally changing.) You may outgrow your friends. New ones will appear.
- Don't worry about people in your past, there's a reason why they didn't make it to your future: *Who matters? Who never did? Who won't anymore? Who always did?*

- You may find after getting into praying more, that you may be confused, sleep more, and have decreased relationship time. Sometimes people sleep for days. This doesn't last long if you don't resist. You're getting ready for a breakthrough. When you come out, you may be born a new person.
- Some things you liked you won't like now. Or things may bother you now that didn't before. You will begin to feel more contented in the mystery world, or spiritual world, than in the real world.
- You may not be able to handle spirituality except in small doses at first. The outrageous message is usually the one from God. You can be angry and protest against God. But you can't be indifferent to God. You can't turn your back on God. (He may want you to feed kids in Ethiopia.)
- Backsliding can happen anytime you left something back there. It's not necessarily negative.
- The hardest thing to do, is to do what you prayed to God would happen. It will take you out of your comfort zone.
- Problems are groupies—there usually isn't just one at a time. But one prayer can affect them all.
- What makes you who you are, is more your struggles than your successes. The Ponderosa Pine needs a forest fire to open its cones to release seeds to grow. Adversity is like that.
- Be patient with yourself. Spirituality doesn't come easy. But it will come. Firewood always shows

up on a river, but we don't know when. And you have to be ready and willing to swim for it.
- God may be rebuilding your house, not your neighbor's. The rebuilding may not be just a matter of fixing up a few things either. It may be a complete teardown, then a total rebuild. You were thinking just a few things needed fixing. But He may be building a palace, because he intends to live in it.
- Sometimes what you thought you wanted, turned out wasn't what you should have wanted. Sometimes God answers prayers by not doing what you ask for. It may not be the answer you wanted, but it may be the answer you needed.

# CHAPTER TWELVE

**IT WILL BE GOOD**

If you accept some spirituality, even just a little, and pray, even just a little…

The curses on your shoulders will begin to lift off.

You'll be free from useless fighting.

If you can't talk your way out of a problem you behaved yourself into, but maybe you can pray yourself out.

Ordinary things will look fresh, as if you're seeing them for the first time.

Paralyzing anxiety over past events will begin to dissipate.

You won't be so likely to impose your values on others.

You'll never tire of a sunset.

You'll begin to see things as they really are

regardless of peoples' opinions.

You'll feel empathy with people from all walks of life.

You'll extend compassion to all other living things.

You'll feel a sense of wholeness and unity with everything and everyone.

You'll feel re-born. Saved from hell on earth.

(You want to experience hell? Try Earth without God.)

All that you lose will be replaced by something better.

When you talk in truth about the past, you will end the story with how you are now. "I was blind but now I see."

You will find that one short simple prayer can instantly heal sick thoughts.

What you put out there will come back to you, whatever it is. What comes around goes around. (There's that cliché thing again.) You will be putting good stuff out there like: bravery, calm, cheer, confidence, giving, delight, hope, relief, sympathy, understanding, serenity… love—you'll receive the same back. People will treat you better and you'll be happier.

You are a creator too. "Thoughts in mind create-like" kind. Go for creating serenity.

*So, after all this:*
You learned all you needed to know to pray…
In the first chapter:

- There are **NO RULES**.
- There are only three parts to a simple prayer:
  **THANKS,**
  **PLEASE HELP,**
  and, **GOD IS GREAT**.
- And you can **BABBLE**

***It's going to be way easier to pray than you thought, isn't it? Why don't you try one now…?***

# AFTERWORD

Some religious practitioners and professionals may take issue with this book. They may fervently believe that prayer must be in a certain format, or through a certain go-between. But God is not bound by the rules of man or religion. When it comes to religions, God must love diversity… because there are *so* many different religions. It is even common for people not to agree with everything their chosen religion professes. Many take what they want and leave the rest.

Everyone is on their own spiritual path with God (and where they are supposed to be on that path). God has many that are not religious. Religion has many that are not God's.

The simple way to pray introduced in this little "how-to" book is not meant in any way to demean or insult any religions. In fact, just the opposite is intended—that is, it has been my goal to help you pray within your chosen belief system. Faith is a learned thing. Most people develop their own idea of what faith is with time. We have been given free will by God to do just that.

But it all boils down to a one-on-one relationship. You and your higher power. And you can communicate directly with your higher power.

I believe God loves diversity. Just look at the animal and plant kingdom. I do not believe that there is just one path to God. I believe there are many, and that they all lead to God.

I have studied all religions looking for common threads. I have traveled the world over. I have visited cultures with no written language and no monetary system. I have prayed under the umbrella of practically every religion there is. I have spun ten-foot-high Buddhist prayer wheels, and hung prayer flags on mountain tops. I have attended charismatic services. I attended classes for two years at the Unity School of Christianity. I have walked the Stations of the Cross. I have spoken in tongues. I have been ordained; I have married and I have buried. I have prayed the rosary in Rome and Paris. I have read the Bible. I have attended Southern Baptist churches and revivals. I have prayed in mosques and at the Western Wall in the old city of Jerusalem. I've studied Shinto in Japan. I've prayed to Allah on an oriental rug barefoot and on my knees in Egypt. I was baptized a Methodist. I've studied the Course In Miracles. I even studied Scientology.

I have been to nearly every Christian-based church the world has to offer. Truly, Christianity is a mansion with many rooms. Some of those rooms are meant to be occupied by you alone. One of the enduring things about Christianity is that it can be individualized and personalized. Christianity preaches fellowship. But it is also the most personal faith path I know.

As the Dalai Lama told me in India, it's better to stay with the faith you grew up with; it's just easier to pray using the structure that you are familiar with as opposed to starting all over.

To some the approach to prayer outlined in this book may appear too bold and presumptuous. The English word *pray* or *prayer* originated from an old French word, which originated from a Latin word *precari*, which meant to ask with humility. So, by strict definition, a prayer is supposed be a humble request, not a demand. The methods of prayer presented in this book may be seen as too demanding and to some... even childish. (Well, we are children.) It may be argued that I advocate approaching God without enough meekness, shyness, or self-effacement.

Well, He'll let you know if you're being too demanding. Besides, that gets into rules. And there are no rules for prayer. Be as bold and as presumptuous as you want. You have nothing to fear. And don't beat around the bush. Say what you feel. Say what you want.

Just ask Him for what you want, give Him his due (praise), and thank Him. It is truly that simple.

Remember, God is always approachable, anytime, anywhere, for any reason—directly, immediately, simply (just be like a child on His lap). There are no rules you have to follow to pray to God. He is simple to talk to. He is there for you.

So... may God bless you with His nearness, understanding, intimacy, and friendship.

Thank You, God, for always being close for us.

You're the greatest!

# APPENDIX ONE

## TOXIC RELATIONSHIPS

Relationships are hard work. Many are failing, have failed, or are just riding the heavy waves of an ocean of misery.

Bad marriages and relationships have common issues outlined below. Not all are in every toxic relationship. They are not in any order of importance. They can differ in degree.

This list provides individuals in difficult relationships specifics to recognize, and then pray for.

Sometimes one has to name the demon.

But remember, everyone is on their own spiritual path (we are human having a spiritual experience), and each of us is where we are supposed to be on our path.

Toxic relationships:

- At the beginning of a new relationship, each person hoped to find their "other half" thereby becoming whole. The new relationship was heady and fun, but was based on wishful thinking, fantasy, and cover-ups.
- Love becomes based on a "picture" of certain expected responses from the other. But as the relationship progresses, instead of satisfying the other's needs, the two individuals become polarized even as the relationship develops into an all consuming entity of its own.
- Each partner's "identity" is based on what they get from the other. The struggle to control can become all-consuming. The failure of one's control over the other may not be recognized.
- What may have been attractive at first may be offensive now. He was the life of the party; she was shy. She was flattered by his attention. She is resentful and jealous now; she expected him to "mature." He expected her to join and enjoy his lifestyle. They may even begin to hate the other for what they originally found lovable.
- As the relationship continues to take on a life of its own (living together, buying things together, common friends, vacations, etc.) the partners begin to feel trapped and stuck. To separate becomes more and more difficult. I-love-you becomes rote and meaningless. They may feel

that they are "living a lie." Sadness and regret fill their hearts instead of love and expectation.
- One partner may be afraid of abandonment or being alone and willingly takes abuse, or just puts up with their partner's annoying idiosyncrasies. Anger, resentment, and frustration smolders inside them.
- One partner may be a "rescuer" driven by a desire to "save" the other. The rescuer tries to make their partner change (manage, manipulate, control), or to fix what is "wrong." The other may obstinately refuse to be "rescued" and in fact may resent the whole process, or actually be mentally ill and needs a doctor's help (which they may refuse to acknowledge). If a partner does not respond to their efforts, the rescuer escalates their efforts, or changes to another tactic. A vicious cycle begins that sucks love from the relationship's "love savings account." The rescuer may defend and help hide the shortcomings of their partner; this is called "enabling."
- One partner may think it's their fault that the other isn't happy. They endlessly and futilely attempt new ways to bring joy to the other. They are plagued by guilt caused by their "failure."
- In toxic relationships the "rules" are forever changing. Each partner feels that they have to "step lightly" or are "walking on eggs." Anything said or done may be taken wrong. Small, normally inconsequential things may tip the balance

causing a blowup. A day can get ruined in an instant, leaving each partner dazed, confused, angry, hurt, and feeling alone or abandoned.
- Many blowups occur just before a social event (don't drink so much, don't flirt, not that dress, my boss, your mother, you forgot the desert, you didn't fix the patio light, etc.) necessitating the couple to pretend to be happy together while still silently communicating their anger from the confrontation. (I'm not happy until you're not happy.) This can cause a deep sadness and barely held-in tears.
- There may be fear (maybe even of physical attack) in toxic relationships. Fear causes a cascade of physiological stressors including sickness, malaise, depression, hypochondria, insomnia, dread, and anxiety. Fear causes defense mechanisms to appear.
- Defense mechanisms attempt to soften the realities of the unpleasant relationship:
  - REPRESSION: Uncomfortable thoughts are pushed away to be dealt with another time. But they simmer.
  - DENIAL: Refusing to accept external reality. Events may be completely discounted or minimized/diluted to make them acceptable. (La-la land.)
  - COMPENSATION: Disguising one's shortcomings (perceived or real) by emphasizing a more positive feature, but not dealing with the shortcoming.

- PROJECTION: The person relegates the blame for their personal shortcomings, mistakes, transgressions, motives, and impulses to the other or another. *It's your fault I'm this way; your mother makes me crazy; your sports addiction makes me crazy.*
- RATIONALIZATION: Justifying actions that otherwise would be unacceptable. These excuses for actions (particularly addictions such as overeating, drinking, smoking, drugs, sexual exploits, etc.) are sincerely believed to be real and justifiable. Of course, they cause guilt and self-effacement.
- REACTION FORMATION: The person fakes a belief opposite of their true belief. They say or do the opposite of what they really want to say or do, sometimes just to keep the peace. This causes internalized anger and frustration. They blame (and even hate) the other for causing them to be something they are not.
- FANTASY: Engaging in daydreams of how things should be rather than doing something about reality. A partner builds a "fictitious" world around friends, parties, volunteerism, avocations, etc. (La-la land.) These are "seen through" by the other partner and resented, or maybe even detested.
- DISPLACEMENT: This is the shifting of an emotion, desire, feeling, dislike, or cause of a discomfort, from the actual object to one more

acceptable, safer, or distant. The substitute may be another family member such as an in-law, or an employer, a friend, a neighbor, a boat... even the family pet.
- ESCAPE: One spends an inordinate time in non-reality—television, reading romances, sports, physical fitness, shopping, crafts, collecting, etc. (More La-la land) This continuously angers and frustrates the partner, sometimes even causing explosive verbal contempt and derision (instantly ruining the day).
- Suffering and sacrifice "bless" all these unions. Each one thinks he or she is sacrificing something to the other and resents the other for it.
- The partners may not consider it bizarre to have both love and hate together in the relationship.
- A sense of duty may bind the partners together (children, business, position, illness, church, circle of friends, etc.) This can be a foundation for hope.
- Toxic relationships force friends to drop away, or the friendships to become shallow. Friends tire of the misery, resentment, criticism, and contempt—the drama. (They may even congratulate you after breaking off the relationship expressing astonishment that it took you so long.)
- Dr. John Gottman, psychologist, known for his work on marital stability and relationship analysis, created what he calls the "Four Horsemen of the Apocalypse" present in toxic relationships. Each

time one appears it's another "nail in the coffin" to the relationship; another little piece of love and caring may be forever gone. Eventually the "love savings account" is empty. The "four horsemen of the relationship apocalypse" are:
- CRITICISM: Attacking the other's personality or character. *You always...; Why are you so...; You never...; You're not being fair.*
- CONTEMPT: Attacking the other's sense of self with abuse, insults, name-calling, hostile humor, sarcasm, mockery, body language, tone of voice, eye-rolling, etc.
- DEFENSIVENESS: Seeing themselves as the victim. They make excuses for themselves or answer a complaint with a complaint; I did this because you did that. Or agreeing at first but then inserting disagreement. Or repeating themselves without acknowledging what the other is saying. Or blaming the other or others.
- STONEWALLING: Withdrawing. Acting neutral but with disapproval. Using tactics such as: icy distance, separation, smugness, stony silence, changing the subject, the "silent-treatment," monosyllabic mutterings, using "the look," or being obstinate.

www.ingramcontent.com/pod-product-compliance
Lightning Source LLC
Chambersburg PA
CBHW072100110526
44590CB00018B/3249